CONTENTS

FUTURE OF INSURING TERRORISM RISKS

TUESDAY, OCTOBER 30, 2001

U.S. SENATE,
COMMITTEE ON COMMERCE, SCIENCE, AND TRANSPORTATION,
Washington, DC.

The committee met, pursuant to notice, at 2:30 p.m. in Room SR–253, Russell Senate Office Building, Hon. Ernest F. Hollings, Chairman of the Committee, presiding.

OPENING STATEMENT OF HON. ERNEST F. HOLLINGS, U.S. SENATOR FROM SOUTH CAROLINA

The CHAIRMAN. The committee will come to order. We are very honored this afternoon to have our distinguished Secretary of Treasury. In that light, I am going to file my opening statement.

[The prepared statement of Senator Hollings follows:]

PREPARED STATEMENT OF HON. ERNEST F. HOLLINGS,
U.S. SENATOR FROM SOUTH CAROLINA

I would like to welcome everyone today's hearing. I would like to extend a special welcome to Treasury Secretary O'Neill for his appearance before the Committee today.

This afternoon, the Commerce Committee will address the need for a national policy and terrorism and other forms of insurance in light of the changes the Sept. 11th terrorist attacks have wrought in the private insurance market.

The problem exists because of insurance companies' threat that they will either cease writing coverages for acts of terrorism unless they receive some relief from the federal government. Given the many key industries that now need terrorism insurance to carry out their vital functions, with the major transportation industries being most significant—airlines, airports, maritime, local port authorities, rail, busing, pipelines—the Congress is compelled to act on this matter.

The question now is not whether the Congress must act, but how? What are the best policy and approach? In acting upon these questions, the principle that we must follow, and the mission that we must stick to—is protecting the American taxpayers from unreasonable risk of exposure. The only way to do this is to ensure that the private market assumes as much responsibility as its capacity will allow it.

The American people already appalled with the level of big business bailouts that are occurring as they on the other hand continue to lose their jobs. The Wall Street Journal—clearly no advocate of liberalism—has raised questions about the economic policies Congress is putting forth. The last thing we must do is push forward a bill that leaves insurance companies on the windfall end and the American taxpayers on the—stuck-with-the-bill-end!

We now know that the Administration has attempted to work out a compromise with the Banking Committee. The agreement purportedly would have the American taxpayers indemnifying 80% of all terrorism damages for the first year, and assuming all damages beyond $10 billion the second and third years, with the hopes the industry will come up with the plan afterwards.

A number of groups, however, have raised doubts about the fairness and prudence of this plan. They claim that it hardly forces the industry to shoulder the financial responsibility of terrorism commensurate with the industry's capacity. The groups that are expressing these concerns range from conservative groups, such as the American Taxpayers Union, to public interest groups, such as the Consumer Federation of America. Some are asking the question as to whether the proposal is too generous for an industry that today has over $300 billion in surplus alone, over $100 billion in reinsurance, in addition to over a trillion in asset worth. We now hear that new entities already are preparing to enter the reinsurance market—thus likely significantly increasing the market's capacity.

This gets to the point of this hearing and the action the Committee plans to take on this issue.

The purpose of this hearing is to hear from the policy experts on how the Congress ought to proceed on addressing the concerns about the private insurance market in the wake of the terrorist attacks. The Administration proposal will be examined, but we also will gather comments on other approaches.

I know an issue of jurisdiction has arisen over this issue. Let the record show, however, that for the past three decades, the Commerce Committee has acted as the Committee of jurisdiction over the business of insurance. It was this Committee that received the legislation introduced in 1980 to amend the McCarran-Ferguson Act. Both in the 102nd and 103rd Congresses, the Commerce Committee was referred legislation to establish broad federal regulation of the insurance industry.

Additionally, through the hard work of Senators Stevens and Inouye, over the past ten years, this Committee has been intensely engaged in efforts to construct a national policy on natural disasters, with the goal of making disaster insurance more available in the marketplace. The Committee's work on that legislation has entailed continuous discussions with state insurance commissioners and the insurance industry. The issues and models that have been put forth to address the issue of disaster insurance are, in essence, similar to the proposals that are being discussed regarding terrorism insurance.

Before closing, I would like to again thank Secretary O'Neill for agreeing to appear to present the Administration's proposal and look forward to working with his Department on this issue.

Senator KERRY.

STATEMENT OF HON. JOHN F. KERRY, U.S. SENATOR FROM MASSACHUSETTS

Senator KERRY. Mr. Chairman, I would like to ask unanimous consent that my full statement be put in the record.

The CHAIRMAN. It will be included.

Senator KERRY. Unfortunately, I cannot stay through the hearing, but I wanted to. Clearly we have to do something, Mr. Chairman. The question is what, is how to structure this. Obviously, if we are going to eliminate any risk-taking by—I mean, the definition of where you have your cut line on what risk you assume within industry and what we risk is the tricky thing here, where you write it.

I suppose one could ask the question in some ways whether the Government is in effect taking over all of that risk or limiting it in some way, that we are in the business, we are going to go on the downside but we are not going to be there on the upside. It is that whole question, and so I am for guaranteeing that people can be insured. Obviously the American economy is going to need the reinsurance capacity, but the question is, Mr. Secretary, where we draw the line and how we do it in a sensible way. Insurance is supposed to reflect risk, and now that risk is much greater, obviously, for something like the World Trade Center or other kinds of things, or perhaps even aircraft in the current mood. You cannot get the insurance, so we need to guarantee that you can, even as we do not assume something that takes away the marketplace itself, I guess is what I am saying.

So Mr. Chairman, I hope we can answer those questions today, and I thank you for having this hearing.

[The prepared statement of Senator Kerry follows:]

PREPARED STATEMENT OF HON. JOHN F. KERRY,
U.S. SENATOR FROM MASSACHUSETTS

Mr. Chairman, thank you for holding this hearing to help our insurance industry maintain our economic stability in the wake of the events of September 11 attacks.

Without access to insurance, future economic activity in the United States is imperiled. I believe we must do everything possible to stabilize the private insurance market and ensure that coverage for terrorism risk is available to businesses and individuals who need it. It is one more action the Congress can take to ensure that terrorists do not win.

The attacks of September 11 have taken important reserves away from the insurance and reinsurance industry and have made it more difficult for the insurance industry to develop prices on terrorism risk insurance. With terrorists attacking our freedom, we must help our insurance and reinsurance companies so they can hold firm and continue offering coverage to their clients. I am disappointed to hear that some reinsurance companies are considering dropping terrorism risk insurance at the end of this year.

Without access to reinsurance, many insurance companies will be unable to offer terrorism risk insurance to its clients next year. This could affect the future economic growth of our nation because access to terrorism risk insurance is vital so that financial institutions can provide financing for businesses, real estate and construction projects. Without access to capital from financial institutions, businesses will have difficulty expanding or even meeting payrolls.

That is why I believe it is important for the federal government to take appropriate action to assist our insurance industry in providing terrorism risk insurance during this crisis. However, I am concerned about a provision of the Bush Administration proposal that would provide new legal procedures to manage and structure litigation arising out of mass tort terrorism incidents. This legislation is likely to be considered on an expedited basis in the Congress. I believe it will be very difficult if not impossible to craft a provision that will ensure that any liability arising from terrorist attacks results from culpable behavior without imposing inappropriate limits on the legal rights of those affected by a terrorist act. Therefore, I do not believe any provision to limit legal action should be included in any insurance aid package.

I look forward to working with the Bush Administration in developing a terrorism insurance proposal that would have the federal government assist insurance companies in paying any significant future terrorism claims. However, as we develop this proposal into legislation, I believe it is important that the federal government provides taxpayer funds as a last resort and only for a limited period of time. It is crucial that the insurance industry continues to be responsible for the risks borne by property/casualty insurance policies. Further, while it will be difficult for insurance companies to develop appropriate prices for terrorism risk insurance, I will strongly object to any company taking this opportunity to gouge their customers or force them to pay rates above what is necessary.

I look forward to hearing the testimony of the witnesses.

The CHAIRMAN. Thank you. Senator Wyden.

STATEMENT OF HON. RON WYDEN, U.S. SENATOR FROM OREGON

Senator WYDEN. Thank you, Mr. Chairman. I will be brief. I think this is an important hearing that you are holding, and I will tell you I have been troubled about the fact that insurance premiums have risen sharply since September 11, even in a number of areas of this country that seem unlikely to be terrorist targets, and what I am particularly hopeful is that the Secretary can spell out today how his approach specifically will help to keep insurance rates down for consumers.

I think it is important that anything Congress does in this area actually translates into more affordable insurance for consumers, rather than just funds that the companies would keep, and so I would just pass this on, Mr. Secretary, by way of saying that this is really in my view central to doing this in the right way.

In addition to that, I think it is important that there be more openness and more accountability with respect to this area than there was in the airline bailout legislation. It is very clear that we are going to be faced with one industry after another coming to the United States Senate asking for assistance, so I come today to listen, and I am certainly anxious to work with the administration in a bipartisan way, but first and foremost I think it is important that this effort spell out how it will help to moderate rates, and the New York Times and others are reporting rates are going up all over the country, even in areas where terrorist acts are unlikely, and then the additional concerns of having openness and accountability are important, Mr. Chairman.

I thank you.

The CHAIRMAN. Senator Boxer.

STATEMENT OF HON. BARBARA BOXER, U.S. SENATOR FROM CALIFORNIA

Senator BOXER. Thank you, Mr. Chairman, and welcome. I also am interested in listening. I want to make a couple of observations that I hope maybe could be answered, Mr. Chairman.

I share what Senator Wyden said about the long-term impact on rates. I also know how effective you have been, Mr. O'Neill, in bringing this issue to our attention. I would like to see the administration be just as strong in terms of helping the people who lost their jobs, because now this would be the second industry, quote-unquote, bail-out, or assistance, but we have not seen, at least I have not seen the same excitement and commitment to do something for the working people who are really struggling with this.

A couple of inconsistencies that I want, or I hope that Mr. O'Neill could discuss is these different signals coming from them that, let us get back to normal, business as usual, go to the World Series, live our life, and yet let us get ready to bail out the insurance companies when the next terrorist attack comes, so if you know something that we do not know in terms of that, I would like to know it.

And then secondly, what I thought was interesting is the National Association of Insurance Commissioners' press release after the recent attacks, that read as follows: Policyholders can rest assured, knowing that the insurance industry in the United States is a $1 trillion industry, with assets of more than $3 trillion. Therefore, and this is their words, preliminary loss estimates of $20 billion represent only 2 percent of the premiums written in 2000, end quote.

Now, having said all of that, I do think the issue of reinsurance is crucial. I mean, if it is not there, it is a problem, but if we are to become a reinsurance company, that is, Uncle Sam, the taxpayers, I would like to see us in essence get some payment from the insurance companies, just like they pay reinsurance companies, and so I think if we are going to take on this role as being a reinsurance company, that means taxpayers, U.S. taxpayers, it should not be a bail-out. It should be a pay-as-you-go situation.

I might close in saying in California we do that with earthquake insurance. The state has stepped in and in fact functions in that fashion, and there are funds that are paid in, and the Government acts as a reinsurance company.

So those are my thoughts, Mr. Chairman. I thank you.

The CHAIRMAN. Thank you. Senator Nelson.

STATEMENT OF HON. BILL NELSON, U.S. SENATOR FROM FLORIDA

Senator NELSON. Mr. Secretary, good to see you again. Mr. Chairman, I just simply want to make one statement, what should be our goal, our challenge here, and it is that we ought to be protecting America's insurance consumers, both corporate and individual, by making sure that the insurance, this terrorism insurance is both available and affordable to protect against these kinds of despicable acts in the future, and so I had an opportunity to testify last week at length on this subject. I am just going to not make any more statements, and get into it as we get into the discussion and the questions.

The CHAIRMAN. One thing, Mr. Secretary, that disturbed the committee, we have been handling insurance matters for my 35 years as a member of this committee, but the administration has never contacted anybody on this committee or myself or the Ranking Member relative to any kind of plan to assist with this terrorism insurance. It looked like an end run by the companies, not by the administration, and in that light I thought it certainly was our responsibility to look into it.

Looking into it, as has been noted, as Senator Boxer said, not a free ride. I just looked at my current issue of Business Week entitled, Giving Insurers a Break But Not a Free Ride, and the administration is not asking underwriters to pay anything for this new terrorism coverage, but the Government should charge insurers premiums for it so that over time insurers will reimburse the U.S. Treasury for any cost, otherwise, in the London Economist, with respect to—and that is, again, October 26, insurance looking up on page 71, after calamity, investors and insurers panic. It happened after Hurricane Andrew struck Florida in 1992, after the Northridge Earthquake wreaked havoc in Los Angeles in 1994, and again after the attacks of September 11, when investors dumped their shares in insurance companies around the world, then all of a sudden the investment mood changed.

The sector has recovered to a level higher than immediately before the attack, and then going on, talking about the hardest hit by the cost of claims were Berkshire Hathaway, Munich Re, Swiss Re, Zurich Financial Services, and AIG, quote, if they can pay their claims, they say, and the share prices of almost all of them have recovered.

So we need to meet not within a panic situation, but within a judicious temperament here to try to make sure, as Senator Nelson has pointed out, that there is affordable, and in making it affordable, the United States government, which does not have jurisdiction over insurance, it is the States has had that for years. Let us be fair about the thing and try to spread the cost amongst the carriers themselves.

With that, let me yield first to Senator Breaux and then Senator Smith.

Senator BREAUX. I will wait.

The CHAIRMAN. Senator Smith.

Senator SMITH. Mr. Chairman, I do not have an opening statement. I am anxious to hear the witnesses.

The CHAIRMAN. Very good. Mr. Secretary, we welcome you.

STATEMENT OF HON. PAUL O'NEILL, SECRETARY, DEPARTMENT OF TREASURY, ACCOMPANIED BY SHEILA BAIR, ASSISTANT SECRETARY FOR FINANCIAL INSTITUTIONS

Secretary O'NEILL. Thank you, Mr. Chairman. It is a pleasure to be here and meet with you and members of the committee. We have, in fact, testified before your colleagues on the Senate Banking Committee and have been meeting with them. In fact, we had a meeting with Chairman Sarbanes and Senator Dodd and Senator Gramm this afternoon that we have been developing the subject, and have also testified in the House, and I welcome this opportunity to appear.

If you do not mind, I would like to introduce Sheila Bair who is sitting here with me. She is an Assistant Secretary at the Treasury Department, and when I was congratulated the other day on how acute my testimony was I had to quickly say, Sheila did it, and so I thought rather than leave the impression that I wrote this myself I wanted you to know Sheila Bair wrote this testimony, which I am very proud to deliver, because I agree with everything that is in it, and I have spent a lot of time thinking about it.

The CHAIRMAN. We are delighted to have her.

Secretary O'NEILL. I have a statement that I would like to submit for the record.

The CHAIRMAN. It will be included.

Secretary O'NEILL. If you do not mind, Mr. Chairman, I have a statement that will take about 10 minutes to work through that I think is worth working through because it addresses some of the issues that have been raised in the first round by the committee, and then go directly to questions.

Mr. Chairman, members of the committee, I appreciate the opportunity to comment on terrorism risk insurance. We believe there is a real and pressing need for congress to act on this issue now. Market mechanisms to provide terrorism risk insurance coverage have broken down in the wake of September 11. Such coverage is now being dropped from casualty and property reinsurance contracts as they come up for renewal. With most policies renewing at year end, if congress fails to act, reinsurers have signaled their intention to exclude such coverage, meaning that primary insurers may have to drop this coverage or institute dramatic price increases.

As a result, after January 1, the vast majority of businesses in this country are at risk for either losing their terrorism risk insurance coverage or paying steep premiums for dramatically curtailed coverage. If businesses cannot obtain terrorism risk insurance, they may be unable to obtain financing or financing may be available only at much higher costs. This would have widespread effects as businesses of all types may, for instance, be unable to expand their facilities or build new facilities.

First, to state the problem as clearly as I know how, and of course you all know this, insurance companies do not take risks. They knowingly accept and mutualize risk. Because insurance companies do not know the upper bound of terrorism risk exposure, they will protect themselves by charging enormous premiums, dramatically curtailing coverage or, as we have already seen with terrorism risk exclusion, simply refuse to offer the coverage.

Whatever avenue they choose, the result is the same, increased premiums and/or increased risk exposure for businesses that will be passed on to consumers in the form of higher product prices, transportation costs, energy cost, and reduced production.

Put another way, any of these choices have the potential to cause severe economic dislocations in the near term, either through higher insurance costs or higher financing costs, and let me say parenthetically that no insurance company would receive a single penny from the federal government if the administration's proposal were to be enacted by the congress. This is not a bail-out bill for the insurance industry that we have proposed. It is, we believe, on the other hand a way to provide for the continuation of insurance coverage for the private sector, by the private sector.

Since September 11, the uncertainty surrounding terrorism risks have disrupted the ability of the insurance companies to estimate, price, and insure the risk. In grappling with this problem, we have had several objectives. First and foremost, we want to dampen the shock to the economy of dramatic cost increases for insurance or curtailed coverage. We also want to limit Federal intrusion into private economic activity as much as possible while still achieving the first objective, and we want to rely on the existing State regulatory infrastructure as much as practicable.

After reviewing an array of options, we developed a plan that we think best accomplishes this objective. This reflects the current evolution of our thinking on this issue and, as I have said to the other committees of congress, we want to work with the congress to achieve the best possible solution, and the way to know when we have achieved the best possible solution will be that the market works. If what we do as a result of our consultations results in legislation that does not permit the existence of a terrorist risk insurance, then we have failed. No one yet knows what those terms will be that will work in the marketplace.

When terrorists target symbols of our nation's economic, political, and military power, they are attacking the Nation as a whole, not a symbol. This argues for spreading the cost across all taxpayers, yet there are also reasons to limit the Federal role. If property owners do not face any liability from potential attacks, they may underinvest in security measures and backup facilities. In addition, the insurance industry has sufficient experience and capacity to price some portion of the risk associated with terrorism and has the infrastructure necessary to assess and process claims.

Under the approach we are suggesting, individuals, businesses, and other entities would continue to obtain property and casualty insurance from insurance providers as they did before September 11. The terms of the terrorism risk coverage would be unchanged and would be the same as that for other risks. Any loss claims resulting from a future terrorist act would be submitted by the policyholder to the insurance company. The insurance company would process the claims and then submit an invoice to the Government for the payment of the uncovered share by the insurance company.

The Treasury would establish a general process by which insurance companies submit claims. The Treasury would also institute a process for reviewing and auditing claims and for ensuring that the private-public loss-sharing arrangement was apportioned among all insurance companies in a consistent manner.

State insurance regulators would also play an important role in monitoring the claims process, and ensuring the overall integrity of the insurance system.

Through the end of 2002, the Government would absorb 80 percent of the first $20 billion of losses resulting from terrorism and 90 percent of insured losses above $20 billion. Thus, the private sector would pay 20 percent of the first $20 billion in losses and 10 percent of losses above that amount. Under this approach, the federal government is observing a portion, but only a portion of the first dollar of losses, which we believe is important to do in the first year of the program.

The key problem faced by insurance companies now is pricing for terrorism risk. We favor a first dollar loss-sharing approach in the first year, because we are concerned about premium increases over the next 12 months. We see this as the best way to mitigate against premium increases, but it may not be the only approach. Again, we are prepared to work with you to find an approach that works in the marketplace.

The role of the federal government would recede over time, with the expectation that the private sector would further develop its capacity each year. In 2003, we would have the private sector be responsible for 100 percent of the first $10 billion, 50 percent of the losses between 10 billion and 20, and 10 percent of the losses above $20 billion. The Government would be responsible for the remainder.

In 2004, the private sector would be responsible for 100 percent of the first $20 billion, 50 percent of losses between $20 and $40 billion, and 10 percent of losses above 40, and the Government would be responsible for the remainder. To preserve flexibility in an extraordinary attack, combined private-public liability for losses under the program would be capped at $100 billion in any year that is left to the congress to determine what to do if payments needed to be or were required to be by experience above $100 billion.

The federal government's involvement would sunset after 3 years. That is to say that we would be out of it.

This approach would also provide certain legal procedures to manage and structure litigation arising out of mass tort terrorism incidents. This includes consolidation of claims into a single form, a prohibition against punitive damages, and provisions to ensure that defendants pay only for noneconomic damages for which they were responsible.

It is important to ensure that any liability arising from terrorist attacks results in culpable behavior rather than overzealous litigation. These procedures are important in mitigating losses arising from any future terrorist attack on our Nation, and are an absolutely essential component of the program that we propose.

Mr. Chairman, for the reasons I have set forth, the administration believes the economy is facing a temporary but nevertheless critical market problem in the provision of terrorism risk insurance. Leaving this problem unresolved we believe threatens our economic stability. The approach that I have outlined limits the Government's direct involvement, retains those elements of our private insurance system that continue to operate well, and provides a transition period to allow the private sector to establish market mechanisms to deal with this insidious new risk that confronts our Nation.

Now I would be pleased to respond to any questions you or the committee may have, Mr. Chairman.

[The prepared statement of Secretary O'Neill follows:]

PREPARED STATEMENT OF THE HONORABLE PAUL H. O'NEILL, SECRETARY OF THE TREASURY

Mr. Chairman, Senator McCain, and Members of the Committee, I appreciate the opportunity to comment on terrorism risk insurance. These hearings are extremely important. We believe that there is a real and pressing need for Congress to act on this issue now. As I will discuss in more detail, market mechanisms to provide terrorism risk insurance coverage have broken down in the wake of September 11. Such coverage is now being dropped from property and casualty reinsurance contracts as they come up for renewal, with most policies renewing at year-end. If Congress fails to act, reinsurers have signaled their intention to exclude such coverage meaning that primary insurers may have to drop this coverage or institute dramatic price increases. As a result, after January 1 the vast majority of businesses in this country are at risk for either losing their terrorism risk insurance coverage or paying steep premiums for dramatically curtailed coverage. This dynamic can in turn be expected to cause dislocations throughout our economy, particularly in the real estate, transportation, and energy sectors.

1. The Problem

The terrorist attacks of September 11 created widespread uncertainty about the risk and potential costs of future terrorist acts. Since September 11, we have endured this uncertainty every day as a country. It has permeated every sector of our economy.

A key part of the government's response to the events of September 11 is to ensure that our economic stability is not undermined by terrorist acts. Continued economic activity is dependent on well functioning financial markets—where the lifeblood of capital is provided to business enterprises. Financial markets allocate capital based on the potential success of a business. In doing so, financial markets rely on the insurance sector to mitigate certain types of risk that are not directly related to the plans or operations of a business.

Insurance companies manage risk in economic activity and facilitate the efficient deployment of capital in our economy by estimating probabilities of possible adverse outcomes, and pooling risk across a large group. Since September 11 the uncertainty surrounding terrorism risk has disrupted the ability of insurance companies to estimate, price, and insure the risk.

We learned on September 11 that, while perhaps highly improbable, terrorists are capable of enormous destruction. Could such an event be repeated? As a country and a government, we are doing everything in our power to prevent a repetition of anything like the events of September 11. But how does an insurance company assess this uncertainty? How does an insurance company price for it? At the moment, there are no models, no meaningful experience, no reasonable upper bound on what an individual company's risk exposure may be.

Insurance companies do not "take" risks. They knowingly accept and mutualize risks. They are private, for-profit enterprises. If they do not believe they can make money by underwriting a particular risk, they will not cover it. Because insurance companies do not know the upper bound of terrorism risk exposure, they will protect themselves by charging enormous premiums, dramatically curtailing coverage, or—

as we have already seen with terrorism risk exclusions—simply refusing to offer the coverage. Whatever avenue they choose, the result is the same: increased premiums and/or increased risk exposure for businesses that will be passed on to consumers in the form of higher product prices, transportation costs, energy costs and reduced production.

The consequences of uncertainties surrounding terrorism risk are already evident in the airline sector. The Department of Transportation's initial projection is that, as a result of the September 11 attacks, airlines will pay nearly $1 billion in premium increases for terrorism risk insurance in the next year despite a congressionally imposed cap on third-party liability. Within the next few months, similar increases can be expected for other forms of economic activity deemed "high risk"—if coverage is available at all. Higher premiums will divert capital away from other forms of business investment.

The need for action is urgent. From our conversations with insurance company representatives, state insurance regulators, policyholders, banks and other entities which provide financing for property transactions, the next two months are critical. The insurance industry relies on a complicated structure of risk sharing. Risk is shared among primary insurers, reinsurers, and retrocessionairs (*i.e.*, providing reinsurance to the reinsurers). This structure has worked well in the past and greatly contributed to widely spreading losses associated with the events of September 11 across the insurance industry.

However, in light of the uncertainty created by September 11, reinsurers have told us that they will no longer cover acts of terrorism in their reinsurance contracts with primary insurers. And as I have said, most property and casualty insurance contracts are up for renewal at year-end. This will create the following choices for insurers: assume all of the risk of terrorism coverage and raise prices to cover all of the associated, unshared costs; reduce coverage levels; or cancel coverage. Any of these choices has the potential to cause severe economic dislocations in the near-term either through higher insurance costs or higher financing costs.

2. Objectives

In grappling with this problem, we have had several objectives.

First and foremost, we want to dampen the shock to the economy of dramatic cost increases for insurance or curtailed coverage. We also want to limit federal intrusion into private economic activity as much as possible while still achieving the first objective. And we want to rely on the existing state regulatory infrastructure as much as practicable.

Note that none of these objectives are directed at providing government assistance to the insurance industry. The industry is absorbing the financial losses it contracted for as a result of the September 11 attacks, and is fully capable of making good on those losses. The industry is also capable of continuing to provide insurance for non-terrorist hazards. The problem, as I have said, is one of uncertainty about future terrorist risk. At the moment, there is no basis upon which to price terrorism risk and no sense of the upper bound on the risk exposure.

3. Options

Over the past few weeks, a variety of proposals have emerged to deal with the problem I have outlined. Before turning to the approach we have developed, I will briefly discuss a few of the alternatives we considered and some of the shortcomings we identified with each.

A case could be made to treat terrorism risk insurance like war risk insurance. During World War II, the federal government provided property owners with insurance protection against loss from enemy attack. Similarly, the Israeli government provides insurance for terrorism risk. This approach would recognize the terrorist threat as one made against all Americans and would establish the broadest possible risk pool for insuring against this risk. At the same time, such an approach implies a permanent federal intrusion in the market so long as any terrorism risk remains.

A second approach, one suggested in various forms by insurance industry representatives, involves the creation of a reinsurance company to pool terrorism risk. This model follows an approach developed in the United Kingdom in response to IRA terrorist activities. This approach has some appeal, especially in providing a vehicle for pooling the industry's risk while providing an upper bound on industry losses through a government backstop. With more time, or in different circumstances, this approach may have been desirable.

In our judgment, however, it has several significant shortcomings. First, the approach ultimately leads to the federal government setting premium rates by establishing the rate charged to the pool for the government's backstop. If the basic problem is that the insurance industry—whose business it is to measure and price risk—

cannot currently price terrorism risk without distorting markets, why would we think the government can do a better job?

Establishing a pool would also take time, and time is very limited since most policies expire at year-end. It is unclear how long it would take industry to capitalize the pool. In the interim, the government's exposure could be substantial, insofar as it would be liable for 100 percent of losses that exceeded the pool's capitalization. In addition, we question whether the government could move quickly enough on its end to establish the contracts, the pricing structure, and the regulatory structure needed to make the proposal work.

Finally, the pool approach creates a federal insurance regulatory apparatus with some presumption of permanence, and a potentially enormous pool of captive capital that we may never need to use. We believe that there will be less uncertainty about terrorism risk a few years from now and that uncertainty will be more manageable by the private sector than is the case today. Given that, why undertake the effort to create a monopoly reinsurer and give a new federal regulator the power to both set prices and regulate insurance companies and their activities?

A third option would be to simply set a large industry deductible and let the federal government cover all losses from acts of terrorism past that point. For instance, the federal government could require the insurance industry to cover all losses up to, say, $40 billion in a given year and the federal government would pay all losses above that amount.

This approach has two substantial drawbacks. First, it does not address the fundamental problem: the industry has no basis for knowing—and hence pricing—terrorism risk. A large deductible would require them to assess premiums large enough to cover a large potential loss. In the absence of better information, we might well expect companies to price insurance as if they fully expected losses up to the deductible amount. Second, this approach makes it difficult to control losses above the deductible as insurance companies would have no incentive to limit costs once their deductible has been paid.

4. A Shared Loss Compensation Program

After reviewing these and other options, and discussing these issues with congressional and industry leadership and the state insurance regulatory community, we developed an approach that we believe best accomplishes the objectives I set forth. Let me say at the outset that this approach reflects the current evolution of our thinking on this issue. We want to work with Congress to achieve the best possible solution. As I have said, the insurance industry can easily protect itself by eliminating coverage or charging very high premiums. What we are trying to do is craft a plan that will prevent the economic dislocations that will otherwise take place if private insurers follow the course they are now on. It is imperative that we find a solution that works in the marketplace. We must get it right, and we must get it right now.

When terrorists target symbols of our nation's economic, political and military power, they are attacking the nation as a whole, not the symbol. This argues for spreading the cost across all taxpayers. Yet there are also reasons to limit the federal role. If property owners do not face any liability from potential attacks, they may under-invest in security measures and backup facilities. In addition, the insurance industry has sufficient experience and capacity to price some portion of the risk associated with terrorism and has the infrastructure necessary to assess and process claims.

Under the approach we are suggesting, individuals, businesses, and other entities would continue to obtain property and casualty insurance from insurance providers as they did before September 11. The terms of the terrorism risk coverage would be unchanged and would be the same as that for other risks.

Any loss claims resulting from a future terrorist act would be submitted by the policyholder to the insurance company. The insurance company would process the claims, and then submit an invoice to the government for payment of its share.

The Treasury would establish a general process by which insurance companies submit claims. The Treasury would also institute a process for reviewing and auditing claims and for ensuring that the private/public loss sharing arrangement is apportioned among all insurance companies in a consistent manner. State insurance regulators would also play an important role in monitoring the claims process and ensuring the overall integrity of the insurance system.

Through the end of 2002, the government would absorb 80 percent of the first $20 billion of insured losses resulting from terrorism and 90 percent of insured losses above $20 billion. Thus, the private sector would pay 20 percent of the first $20 billion in losses and 10 percent of losses above that amount.

Under this approach the federal government is absorbing a portion—but only a portion—of the first dollar of losses, which we believe is important to do in the first year of the program. The key problem faced by insurance companies right now is pricing for terrorism risk. While this type of loss sharing approach does not completely alleviate that problem, it does provide insurance companies with the ability to evaluate potential losses on a policy by policy basis, with clearly defined maximum exposures. For example, on a $100 million commercial policy the insurance company's maximum exposure would be $20 million. If industry losses were greater than $20 billion that exposure would be reduced even further.

More importantly, price increases to policyholders should be lower under this approach than under an approach that requires companies to absorb 100 percent of losses up to a large, aggregate industry loss deductible. Under this approach, if an insurance company's maximum exposure was defined at $20 million on a $100 million policy, the insurance company could then price that $20 million exposure on the probability of a complete loss event occurring.

Suppose instead that the insurance industry had to absorb $20 billion in losses before any government loss sharing began. Then, in our example, the insurance company's maximum loss exposure would be $100 million on that policy, not $20 million. Pricing to this maximum loss would create the economic dislocation we are trying to avoid.

The role of the federal government would recede over time, with the expectation that the private sector would further develop its capacity each year. As private sector capacity increases, the nature of the government's loss sharing agreement would also change. Given more time and experience, we believe that the insurance industry could reestablish robust risk-sharing arrangements such as reinsurance that would enable the private sector to insure losses from terrorism before the government loss sharing commenced.

Thus, in 2003, we would have the private sector be responsible for 100 percent of the first $10 billion of insured losses, 50 percent of the insured losses between $10 and $20 billion, and 10 percent of the insured losses above $20 billion. The government would be responsible for the remainder.

In 2004, the private sector would be responsible for 100 percent of the first $20 billion of insured losses, 50 percent of the insured losses between $20 and $40 billion, and 10 percent of the insured losses above $40 billion. The government would be responsible for the remainder.

To preserve flexibility in an extraordinary attack, combined private/public liability for losses under the program would be capped at $100 billion in any year. It would be left to Congress to determine payments above $100 billion.

The federal government's involvement would sunset after three years. It is our hope, indeed our expectation, that the market problem we face today will have been corrected by then so that the private sector will be able to effectively price and manage terrorism risk insurance going forward. Of course, should that prove not to be the case, Congress and the President can reevaluate the program in place and decide at that time on an extension of the program or establishment of some other approach.

This approach would also provide certain legal procedures to manage and structure litigation arising out of mass tort terrorism incidents. This includes consolidation of claims into a single forum, a prohibition on punitive damages, and provisions to ensure that defendants pay only for non-economic damages for which they are responsible. It is important to ensure that any liability arising from terrorist attacks results from culpable behavior rather than overzealous litigation. These procedures are important to mitigating losses arising from any future terrorist attack on our nation, and are an absolutely essential component of the program I have outlined.

Finally, this approach requires a clear definition of an "act of terrorism." We suggest that the Secretary of the Treasury, with the concurrence of the Attorney General, and in consultation with other members of the Cabinet, be given authority to certify that a terrorist act had taken place for purposes of activating the shared loss compensation arrangement.

We believe that this approach dampens any adverse economic impact from a sudden increase in the cost from terrorism risk insurance over the next 12 months. The imposition of a deductible in the second year, and an increase in the deductible in the third year, permits the federal government to gradually withdraw from the market as the private sector adapts to measuring and pricing terrorism risk.

5. Conclusion

Mr. Chairman, for the reasons I have set forth, the Administration believes that the economy is facing a temporary, but critical, market problem in the provision of terrorism risk insurance. Keeping our economy moving must be our overriding concern. Leaving this problem unresolved threatens our economic stability. The approach I have outlined limits the government's direct involvement, retains all those elements of our private insurance system that continue to operate well, and provides a transition period to allow the private sector to establish market mechanisms to deal with this insidious new risk that confronts our nation.

There are no perfect solutions to this problem. We have developed what we believe is a sound approach. As I explained earlier, we do not believe that creation of a reinsurance pool can be accomplished under the time constraints we face, but we would be glad to explore modifications to our approach with the Committee.

I would be pleased to answer any questions the Committee may have.

The CHAIRMAN. Well, Mr. Secretary, you say it is not a bail-out, but what will the government be paid, or how will the government be paid for this particular approach?

Secretary O'NEILL. Well, they would not be paid at all, and we would not have given the industry anything at all, except, in effect, a clear declaration to the industry and to people who buy insurance that in the event they are struck by a terrorist act, that they will not be forced to suffer a 100 percent loss, and we have proposed, in order to keep the insurance industry in this process that their exposure to liability be limited, and if I may, with the structure we have proposed, with industry exposure for 20 percent of the first $20 billion, the aggregate exposure for the insurance industry up to $20 billion would be $4 billion.

Now, none of us know, no one knows how to put a risk premium on a terrorist act, because the way insurance prices are set now is by experience and by the collection of statistical data that reflects an anticipated rate of experience of something happening. We can do this for age for life insurance, and we can do it from automobile insurance from knowing crashes that occur. We can even do it for hurricane. The chairman knows this very well from his own State's exposure to hurricanes and others of you have had tornadoes and earthquakes and the rest.

We have enough experience that the insurance industry knows how to put a premium price on all kinds of events. Thank God, we do not have enough experience to put a price on terrorist events, and so one of the options that we looked at was to say, since this is effectively for the moment, and hopefully forever, an unpriceable event, we could consider saying that if an event is determined to be in a terrorist event, it should accrue to the cost structure of the American people, which is to say, we the people of the United States.

Rather than do that when we show the President all of the options, he decided we should put forward this 80/20 proposal, which we know does something very important. It keeps the insurance industry in the business of assessing risk and working with individual companies to tend to the questions of whether individual companies are making the proper level of investment to reduce the risk that is associated with the way that they conduct their business.

Second, in the event there is a terrorist act and a claims process, having the insurance companies involved gives us that front line of engagement of people who are trained in assessing the cost that should be paid out as a consequence of the loss, and with our 80/20 proposal up to 20 billion, we believe the insurance industry can figure out how to collect premiums to cover their risk exposure up to $20 billion.

It is not the usual way one would price insurance premiums, but it has the virtue of keeping the companies in. It costs the government nothing to do and so we think that this is a way to proceed, and the reason we are concerned is, frankly, it is not because we have a burning heart for the insurance industry, but because in many, many business situations, if a business cannot get coverage for all kinds of risk, including the risk of terrorist acts, their financial backers are either not going to give them the money they need for expansion or continuation, or the financing cost is going to affect insurance premium, which the lender will in effect put into his own price to the borrower.

And we think the danger of being in a position when 70 percent of today's property and casualty coverage comes up for renewal on January 1 with no provision at the moment, or appearance on the horizon of property and casualty insurance with a terrorist risk provision, we think we run a great danger of causing chaos in the financing arrangements between those who are investing and those who wish to invest, because there is no assurance of coverage against this kind of catastrophic loss.

The CHAIRMAN. But you say at no cost to the government?

Secretary O'NEILL. Right.

The CHAIRMAN. How do you figure that? That is wonderful. That is the first I have ever heard of up here that does not cost us. Where are we going to get the money? I mean, you say you are not charging the companies, not even a premium so that they can over the years subsist, as you say, and survive and continue in business, and then pay it back, but you do not have a charge.

Secretary O'NEILL. Senator, under our plan the companies will go out and they will sell insurance at premiums that cover their potential loss.

The CHAIRMAN. How about our loss?

Secretary O'NEILL. Let us think about the terrorist risk insurance. All the risk belongs to the American people. Now, you could say, well, it does not really belong to the American people, because we are going to turn a blind eye to those who do not have terrorist insurance, and it is just too bad if you have a billion-dollar building in Chicago and it is lost, and we have not done anything to create a mechanism for some terrorist risk insurance.

We could say it belongs to the property owners of America. We think that will raise the cost of doing business in the United States, because the financial community in effect will impose more than a traditional insurance cost to assure that they do not lose all of their money because the property buyer or the group that is on its way to earning an equity position in the property, if they cannot assure the lender that they are going to be able to pay the money back in the face of a terrorist loss, they are not going to provide the money at the same cost, and so the cost of financing our society is going to go up to reflect this loss of capacity.

The CHAIRMAN. I have an order of appearance as Senator Nelson, Wyden, Boxer, Breaux, Smith, Inouye, and Dorgan, who is really the chairman of this subcommittee. Let me yield, then, to Senator Nelson.

Senator NELSON. Thank you, Mr. Chairman.

Mr. Secretary, you have outlined the position of the administration that you had presented last week. Are you presently under discussions with members of the Senate about a compromise that would basically eliminate year 1 of your proposal and instead insert a $10-billion retention level up to which the companies would have to absorb that as part of their terrorism risk insurance?

Secretary O'NEILL. I said earlier, indeed, I just this afternoon have spent another hour with members of the Banking Committee to talk about how we can do something quickly. I frankly feel the most important thing is that the congress act quickly.

I said earlier no one knows what will work yet in the marketplace. I am frankly skeptical that starting off the first year with $10 billion will work, but I do not have any evidence to present to you except my own 25 years worth of experience in private sector being a buyer of insurance and knowing what insurance cost does to the total cost of products, and knowing what risks are associated with not being able to get coverage against terrorists unless you are a very big company with very deep pockets, and so I have said yes, we are working with the committee, and yes they are talking about a 10 billion dollar deductible, and yes I have doubts whether the market will take it. We will find out. If the market will not take it we are going to have to do something else or accept responsibility for adding a very big cost of doing business in the United States, which is another penalty for the United States economy.

Senator NELSON. It has been my experience in dealing with with insurance companies that the best way to have the private sector is for the insurance companies to stay in the game, and in the proposal that you have outlined, the maximum exposure that the company would have in the first year is $4 billion. We are talking about a P and C industry that has a surplus in the range of $300 to $350 billion, and so we are talking about not anywhere close to tapping what this industry's surplus is.

Tell me, what is your philosophy of why you would not want the insurance companies to stay in the game? The only way, having to accept that risk responsibility, and then for the gargantuan type of terrorism loss, that the federal government would step in in some form or fashion there.

Secretary O'NEILL. Senator, I am a businessman temporarily on leave to be a public servant, and so let me tell you my answer as a businessman. Insurance companies are like all other kinds of companies. They have a requirement to earn the cost of capital. Those who do not earn the cost of capital over time go out of business, and they are not businessmen or businesswomen any more, they are failures, and so at least for me, it helps me to be really clear about what business is all about.

Now, it is true that the insurance companies have reserves. Why do they have reserves? Because under State laws—and you know this as a former insurance commissioner—insurance companies that write insurance are required to have reserves so that if and when, as often is the case, they are called on to pay the claims that are associated with coverage they agree contractually to provide, so that when we show up with a broken car or someone dies they pay off. That is why the reserves are there, and for no other reason.

Now, one could say the reserves have been permitted to get too big and they are earning too much money on the reserves. That is a separate conversation. It may be a worthy conversation, but it has nothing whatsoever to do with the question of whether we should have this kind of mechanism or not, and if we should have this kind of mechanism, they are going to have to have reserves to pay off these claims.

The reason I am worried about the $10 billion deductible that we are talking about with the Senate Banking Committee is this. If you think about what this means from an insurance company or an insurance industry point of view, when we say they should be responsible for 20 percent of the first $20 billion, and then we say, and then they should be responsible for $10 billion on top of that, we are really saying we want the insurance industry to go out there and collect premiums in the amount of $14 billion, because in order for them to protect themselves against loss—and let me say again, insurance companies do not take risk, they mutualize the risk, and so if they are on the hook for the potential of $14 billion, only an idiot would not go out and collect enough premiums to pay the exposure that is associated with the terrorist risk, and so they will go out and collect the premium.

Now, as I said before, we do not know how to put an actuarial value on these premiums, because we only have one experience of this kind, and it could very well be—hopefully it will be we never have another terrorist example like this one, and so if we put a $14 billion premium charge out there that has got to be collected by the insurance industry and there is never another terrorist event, through our legislative action we have created a $14-billion gift for those who wrote the insurance, who then did the logical thing and went out and collected the premiums, so the more you want to penalize the industry, the bigger the premiums, the less likely that it is actually going to work. In the event that we do not have a terrorist event, the more money you have, in fact, created for the insurance industry.

Senator NELSON. Mr. Chairman, by the logic of the Secretary—and I respect your opinion, but I just respectfully disagree. By your logic, your governmental proposal is to let them go out and charge a premium for the $14 billion that you say they may be liable for while at the same time letting that be on a shared basis with the U.S. Government doing 80/20 on the first $20 billion, when in fact the last time I checked, insurance companies were supposed to be in the business of assuming the risk.

Now, we have never anticipated these kinds of catastrophic risks until we had to face what we did in Florida with Hurricane Andrew and a $16 billion insurance loss, and now we have a new kind of catastrophic risk, and what I would respectfully recommend to the committee is that as we grapple through something very, very difficult, that you have got to keep the insurance companies in the game, functioning as insurance companies with States insurance regulators looking over their shoulder checking their premiums, and then for the real catastrophic rise above a certain figure, that the federal government would participate in some way, either direct grants, or loans, or whatever the committee devises, but that is just my 2 cents, and I look forward, Mr. Chairman, to following this discussion.

The CHAIRMAN. Senator Wyden.

Senator WYDEN. Thank you, Mr. Chairman. What really generated my opening remarks, Mr. Secretary, was that survey that was done by the New York Times and others saying that since 11 September insurance premiums have soared in places that are extremely remote.

In fact, the New York Times said with respect to the increases, quote, far from being limited to cities and companies that seem most vulnerable, the rising rates are reaching into the quietest, most remote areas of the country, so clearly mom and pop companies in rural America are being hit in a way that has no relation to terrorism.

What would your plan do to if not completely reverse that, at least stabilize it so that people would see that this was truly related to terrorism?

Secretary O'NEILL. Senator, I am sure you know that traditionally and historically the insurance industry has been regulated at the state level, and our proposal would in no significant way change that regulatory process. We would leave it at the State level.

Again, as one who has bought a lot of insurance from a company point of view, the best friend of a consumer is competition, and it may very well be that there are some rate increases in the wake of what we saw on September 11, and the way that those rates will come down is with competition.

Most of what we are seeing so far is increases in property and casualty insurance that will be taken out by competition, but it will take some time. If you go in and look at other catastrophic events that we have had like this, the insurance industry is one where, if they do not collect enough premiums to pay for all of their losses, they will raise the premiums in the next round in anticipation of another event, and the survivors will collect enough premiums to pay the cost.

Insurance companies—believe me, insurance companies do not lose money and stay in business.

Senator WYDEN. I am all for competition. It is just in these rural areas there really is not much competition, and you see particularly with these mom and pop firms that their increases do not seem related to risk, which leads me to my second question.

In your view, what is the fundamental problem you want to see the United States Senate deal with? Is it that the current risk of terrorist events is too large for the industry to have, or is it that the risk of terrorism is too difficult to price?

Secretary O'NEILL. I think we need to think about multiple objectives. I think it makes a lot of sense to keep the insurance industry in place and working with companies of all sizes to help companies take the investment actions and develop practices that will reduce risk as much as possible related to terrorist events, and I think when a company has an insurable relationship, has an insurance relationship, it works with companies to reduce risk, and I think that is very valuable, and as I said earlier, I think in the event there is another catastrophe, having the insurance company out there assessing claims and helping to pay claims is a really valuable thing to do, and getting the right valuation up front on the value of property that might be total losses is a very useful thing. We have no capacity to do that in the Federal Government. It would take an unbelievable amount of time to develop a parallel capacity to what exists in the private sector.

Senator WYDEN. That leads me to my last question. You are saying this really relates to valuations, it relates to prices, it relates to financial terms. Insurance companies tell political risk insurance, for example, which covers multinational companies against the risk of political turmoil in foreign countries. I mean, they seem to sell insurance in a variety of instances where it is fairly hard to make calculations.

Is it your sense that this is largely a temporary problem, and that if the United States Senate was back here in a year or two that the industry would have figured out terrorism pricing?

Secretary O'NEILL. I hope so. If you had had a hearing on this subject 2 months ago, or 3 months ago, the industry would have told you that they are providing terrorist risk coverage, and they were. I mean, the policies, many policies did not have any exclusion, but they realized after the event that they had not really believed that anything like the World Trade Center could happen, and so an industry person would tell you it is a completely new set of facts that they have got to deal with. They can deal with hurricanes, they can deal with tornadoes, they can deal with earthquakes, because there is some level of predictability, but willful acts of evil people is not something the insurance industry has traditionally had a probability series that it could apply to casualty losses and give you a premium number.

Senator WYDEN. Mr. Chairman, I would wrap up simply by saying that I think, Mr. Secretary, what you have done is made the case for what Senator Nelson and I and others are calling for, and that is the federal government should not be picking up 80 percent of the losses from the first dollar of those losses incurred, because you have just said the industry is really going to sort this out, and I would hope that as we go through this, and we are going to work with you, then instead of picking up such a big chunk of the cost from the very first dollar out, that in effect the Government is regarded as a backstop. We are essentially a backstop out there for extraordinary losses when the private sector in effect is not working, and I hope we can work with you towards that end.

Thank you, Mr. Chairman.

The CHAIRMAN. Senator Boxer.

Senator BOXER. Mr. Chairman, thank you. I want to be helpful here and I want to be sensible and I want to do the right thing, but I am extremely troubled by something you said, and help me get through it. If I misinterpreted, let me know.

You said only an idiot would not go out and collect premiums to cover the risk, but yet you are asking the Federal Government to in a sense be idiots, because we are at risk for untold billions of dollars, and there is nothing in your plan that we collect premiums to cover our losses, and so in that statement that you made, I think you are putting taxpayers in a position of being idiots, and I am not going to let it happen, to be honest with you.

I want to be helpful, I am willing to be helpful, but just to say we are going to pick up a portion of the first dollar losses—and you said two other things. You said twice—you said it in different ways. You said, this plan of the administration's costs the government nothing, and then you said, insurance companies will get nothing. Well, I hope you are right. Under your plan, if nothing happens, that is right, but yet your plan says that government will pick up untold billions, no cap on that. Am I correct, if something happens next week or next year, or the next couple of years, wouldn't the government have to pay in that case if there were tens of billions of dollars of losses?

Secretary O'NEILL. Maybe it would be helpful to work through a specific example, and maybe to do it, let us take the World Trade Center, and just use some rough numbers, and let us roll the clock back and say, now, the experience of these awful acts, I have a $4 billion building, and let me be the owner of the building first, and I have financing lines and insurance companies and other people have invested in backing me, and I borrowed the money because I am going to be able to make enough money with the occupancy that I am going to make a 15-percent rate of return on my money, all right, and before this event I was able to get coverage, property and casualty coverage for—let us say for $100 million a year.

After this event, and I have still got a $4 billion building, let us say, and there is now knowledge in the world of this experience, and I go to the insurance company and they say, I am not going to write you terrorist coverage any more, and my bankers say, and I am not going to loan you money so you can have this building. Maybe we go through bankruptcy until we find, maybe there is an individual in the world with $4 billion that does not need to have banking relationships or insurance relationships, and the building ends up with that person, but short of that there is no owner for this building, because it cannot be financed. It cannot be financed because I cannot get insurance.

Senator BOXER. I totally understand the problem. That is why we are here, and you are right, we have a problem. The question is the solution to the problem, and that is where you lose me when you say, again, only an idiot would not go out and collect premiums to cover the risk, and I think that is where we have taxpayers in a position, if we follow your leadership, and the administration's leadership on this, I look at it as taxpayers are on the line for untold billions, and there is no source of revenue coming in to help us. How is that fiscally responsible for us?

I mean, if we are going to be the insurer of last resort, and we just say, we are there for you, without having some kind of a businesslike plan, that is the issue.

I totally get what you are saying, and that is why I want to be helpful, but I am just identifying myself with my colleagues who say at this point, the plan that we see before us is very troubling as far as the taxpayers of this country are concerned, and I think that your comments that you made here today even underscore it, absolutely.

How many times have Republicans said, and Democrats, we need to run the government more like a business? We need to run the government more like a business and be smart and not put ourselves out on the line like this, and that is what is concerning me. I hope we can work together toward a bill that I think gives taxpayers some more protection than the current plan.

Secretary O'NEILL. May I finish my example, Mr. Chairman? If I am sitting there with a $4 billion building and you are an insurance company now, and I insist that I want you to provide terrorist coverage for me, your premium to me, if you believe that this is an unknowable event, is $4 billion a year, and that is not payable for me.

Senator BOXER. I understand the problem.

Secretary O'NEILL. So I am fundamentally out of business, and so if you would like for me to pay my $4 billion to the insurance company and to the federal government, it does not really help me with my investment.

Senator BOXER. No, I was not suggesting that. I was just suggesting that if we are going to be in the business of backing all this up, we should not be idiots, and we should follow your leadership on that point just as insurance companies are going to go out and say, well, we will pick up everything. I understand the problem, but we can have an insurance pool just as we have in California, and it is functioning very well so far, because the risk is spread and you do not have to pay $4 billion in reinsurance, even though you may get hit really hard.

So I just want to work with you, because I think what you have got on the table is unfair to taxpayers, exceedingly fair to insurance companies. I want to help them, but I just do not think it is a checks-and-balances type of situation.

The CHAIRMAN. Senator Breaux.

Senator BREAUX. Thank you very much, Mr. Chairman, for having the hearing, and thank you, Mr. Secretary. The fact is, I think the American taxpayer is going to be picking up the cost of these terrorist acts several times over. I mean, through charitable contributions and fundraisers, through the money that this Congress is appropriating to cover the losses in New York, the tax incentives, we are going to be adopting in order to encourage businesses to stay in New York, or to locate in New York, to make sure that the economy survives, I mean, the taxpayer in fact is going to be putting out a great deal of money because of the acts of the terrorists. It is a question of how we do it.

I think history is going to be an important lesson as we all, I think, would agree, and I was interested in your comments about World War II and what this country did under President Roosevelt in World War II. I do not remember. Our distinguished chairman probably remembers that time.

It seems that what you are saying is that the Congress at that time passed legislation which basically insured and picked up 100 percent of the loss for terrorist attacks against our merchant ships, even before the war. Is that what we did then?

Secretary O'NEILL. Senator, that is my understanding. In fact, I do not think we provided insurance. We agreed that the American people would cover the cost through our agreed system of taxes.

Senator BREAUX. I take it at that time, companies that had merchant ships had commercial insurance, but I guess we made a decision that that insurance was either not able to cover terrorist attacks or just was not the right thing, so the Government just picked up the whole cost.

Secretary O'NEILL. Exactly.

Senator BREAUX. Is there any distinction in the suggestion from the administration as to any differences between foreign terrorists and domestic terrorist attacks?

Secretary O'NEILL. What we are proposing would have effect only inside the geographic boundaries of the United States, but the origin of the act would not distinguish among those who might have committed the act

Senator BREAUX. And there would have to be a certification?

Secretary O'NEILL. There would have to be a certification of a terrorist event having taken place.

Senator BREAUX. How can we price the cost of this insurance you are talking about, the fact that if the insurance companies have 100 percent of the risk against terrorist attacks, that is something that you really cannot price because of the uncertainty of it? Well, if that is true for 100 percent of the cost, why is it not just as true for 20 percent of the cost? Isn't the basic problem the same, that you cannot put a cost on 100 percent? How can you put a cost on the first 20 percent?

Secretary O'NEILL. Senator, you are absolutely right, and that is why we have tried to limit in what we have done the upper level of exposure to those who are going to write these policies, because as I said earlier, they are going to go out and they are going to price their premiums at a level that covers their full exposure, and so the more we think we are putting their skin in the game, or causing them to be part of this, the more we are insisting in effect on the buyers of these policies pre-budgeting the unknown cost of the terrorist act.

Senator BREAUX. Well, I do not want anybody to be unjustifiably be compensated, or reimbursed, or unjustifiably make money out of these terrorist activities. I do not think anyone in the congress or the administration is aimed at doing that.

The fact is, the taxpayer and this congress is going to be spending a great deal of money for the cost of terrorism. We are going to be funding a lot of things. We are going to be reimbursing a lot of losses to cities, and we are going to do that basically on a 100-percent reimbursement rate, and I think everybody agrees that is the right thing to do, because we are a country, regardless of where we are from and what State we are from.

I just think that we ought to be very careful that in doing that, in guaranteeing that the insurance would be there, that we are not somehow creating a situation where some industry or business unjustifiably is compensated or benefits from that, and I would hope that we would make sure that whatever you propose does not allow that to happen.

Thank you, Mr. Chairman.

The CHAIRMAN. Thank you. Senator Smith.

Senator SMITH. Thank you, Mr. Chairman. Mr. Secretary, thank you for being here.

Why should we pay the first dollars, 20 percent of $80 billion. Why can we not pay the last portion of that, to be the backstop, as some of my colleagues have talked about?

Secretary O'NEILL. All right, let us conceptualize a different approach. Let us say that the federal government should be there only after we have experienced $50 billion worth of losses.

From a point of view of an individual buyer of insurance, and from the point of view of insurance companies, as they come together to write insurance coverage for the terrorist loss they are going to end up with prices we think are going to be staggering increases in prices for the privilege of having insurance, because to the degree that we put our contribution in, or our participation at higher and higher levels, we are leaving all the ground between zero and whatever magic number you want for the private sector to mutualize through premiums.

So, for example, if I were still where I was, and I had lots of billion dollar plants, and one of those plants might be the subject of a kamikaze attack, then my risk is really the whole billion-dollar plant to a terrorist act, and from an insurance company point of view, if you think there is a high probability that it is officially visible and damaging to the American economy that you are really at risk for the billion dollars, you are either going to not sell me insurance, or you are going to charge me a premium that is staggering to my total cost.

Senator SMITH. But are we not just speculating now?

Secretary O'NEILL. We are, absolutely.

Senator SMITH. Are you hearing from banks that they are not going to make operating loans to businesses unless they have terrorist insurance?

Secretary O'NEILL. In fact, what I am hearing from the insurance industry in this country and around the world is basically saying, count us out, and last week I had lots of business people in town for a variety of meetings, and so I made a practice of asking some of those I saw, tell me about what is happening with your insurance.

One person from Chicago has a $600 million office building, and he told me his policy, like most insurance policies, are subject to renegotiation at the call of either the insured or the insurer, certainly within a relatively short period of time, usually a year. His policy had been called. His rates had been tripled for property and casualty, and his terrorist risk insurance had been taken out of his policy.

Senator SMITH. Won't he just go bare?

Secretary O'NEILL. He is big enough to do it. He is big enough to do it. You know, the people who—except for one thing, which I quickly said to him, the fact that he goes bare will be noted by S&P and Moody's. These are the rating agencies, and they will say, we, the shareholders, or proxies for shareholders, now have a new $600 million hole in our protection against a catastrophic loss and we are going to lower your bond rating so that your financing cost goes up to reflect, in effect, the insurance premium that you are not paying, so do not think you can escape this evil thing that is going to happen to you. It will be reflected. The finance system grinds very finely. It will find all the tricks. There are no ways to avoid this problem.

Senator SMITH. And do you think if we do not act on this, that we are contributing to this recession in some way? Do you think this is important to be part of a stimulus package?

Secretary O'NEILL. I think we run an untold and uncertain risk, but I do not think there is any doubt that we could do substantial damage to the thrust of the economy if we turn off investment on 1 January because so many businesses are unable to get financing because they cannot get terrorist insurance.

Senator SMITH. Since we are speculating here, do you have in your proposal any kind of a sunset, and what is that?

Secretary O'NEILL. We propose, Senator, that this go on for 3 years, that as time goes, that over the second and third year we would lower the federal participation. I have to tell you frankly we do not know whether that is workable. It is a set of ideas about how we think to proceed. The critical thing is what is available on January 1 and for 12 months, because that is the basis on which insurance policies are conventionally written, for 1 year, and the terms will be established or not established as a reference from whatever legislation you all enact.

Senator SMITH. Mr. Chairman, I assume the point of that phase-out is that we will have some pricing history then that allows the marketplace to get in there.

Thank you, Mr. Chairman.

The CHAIRMAN. Let the record show, insurance shares looking up, surprising beneficiaries of terrorism, and I am reading the overall cost for insurers are now put at $35 to $41 billion. According to estimates by Morgan Stanley, those hit by costly claims are likely to include Berkshire Hathaway, Munich Re, Smith re, Zurich Financial Services, and AIG. They can pay their claims, they say, and the share prices of almost all of them have recovered, rather than everybody out, that you just attested to.

Senator INOUYE.

Senator INOUYE. I believe all of us agree that since we have not had any experience with so-called acts of terrorism that insurance industry provided casualty and property but no terrorism coverage.

Having said that, even without the experience under your proposal you will have to certify that this was an act of terrorism and this was not, and I think there is a lot of confusion, not among the experts, but among people in general, because we do not refer to this as terrorism. We say, this is war here, war there, war everywhere. What is your definition of an act of terrorism? Would the letter that Senator Daschle received be an act of terrorism or an act of war?

Secretary O'NEILL. This is dangerous territory, especially to deal with specific examples. What we have done in the past—and let me go back to what Senator Breaux was saying. In the past, we have had a declaration of war, and we were able then to say this is an act of war or this is not an act of war. We are in wholly new territory here, and one of the big challenges is writing a testable and hopefully lasting definition of terrorism, which is something we need to do with you all.

Would I say in a general sense that the letter to Senator Daschle is an act of terrorism? Yes, but I am not sure that I would want that to be the centerpiece of how we write terrorism insurance, because I want to write it for property and casualty as the main line of what we are trying to do, because I think that is where the biggest risk is, is that we are going to have the absence of coverage for property and casualty insurance.

Some of these other areas are much more difficult to deal with. For example, one could ask why should life insurance not be subject to some sort of special provision related to terrorism? I do not have an answer for you. Again, this is wholly new territory that we are moving into here.

Senator INOUYE. Would Oklahoma be considered an act of terrorism?

Secretary O'NEILL. I am sorry.

Senator INOUYE. The Oklahoma federal building.

Secretary O'NEILL. I would say yes. In that case, it was self-insured, because it was a governmental building.

Senator INOUYE. How far would your coverage be in the case of New York?

Secretary O'NEILL. Well, what we have said in our recommendation for the congress to consider is a cap of $100 billion to proceed under this scheme. In the conversations we have been having with the Banking Committee and with the committee in the House there have been arguments on both sides of either reducing the $100 billion or taking the limit off completely, and there are arguments for doing a host of different things. The scale of New York is—I do not really think we know yet, $40 or $50 or $60 billion, perhaps, and so again I do not think you can make our conceptual arguments at $100 billion, that that is enough, without some sort of a cap.

Again, if you agree to keep the private sector in it means that however small their share of the risk, it is the risk to infinity if you do not have a cap, and so that is a consideration, because again it will affect the premiums that they feel they have to charge in order to insure their sliver of infinity.

Senator INOUYE. I realize that, for an economy to continue in a viable fashion, these losses would have to be covered one way or the other, whether it is by the industry or by the Government, or combined, but my colleagues will cover the technical aspects. I am just curious, when the time comes, you will have to decide, will you not, as to what is terrorism?

Secretary O'NEILL. Unfortunately, that is right.

Senator INOUYE. And you will have to decide whether the Daschle letter was an act of terrorism, but at this moment you are not prepared to do so?

Secretary O'NEILL. No. I would like to have the benefit of working with all the members of the congress who need to be involved in this process, and with your staff experts, and with the people, the experts outside so that we approximate as best we can a solution that will work in the marketplace.

Senator INOUYE. Thank you very much.

The CHAIRMAN. Senator Dorgan.

Senator DORGAN. Mr. Chairman, thank you very much.

Mr. Secretary, thank you for being here. I think the question is not whether something needs to be done, but the question is how do we do it, and my guess is from your testimony and from other things that I have reviewed that the new and previously unanticipated risk that now exists in the marketplace renders the marketplace incapable of dealing with it otherwise. All of us believe the marketplace is a pretty good allocator of goods and services, but the marketplace at this point cannot work under these circumstances, is that your point?

Secretary O'NEILL. It is our view that if we do not do something like what we have proposed, that there is not going to be a reinsurance pool after January 1 for terrorist risk insurance, and therefore there will not be any terrorist risk insurance, and as a consequence we will do substantial, if not great damage to the momentum of our economy, because people who want to make investments or continue with the ones we have will not be able to secure financing at all, or for sure at the same rates that they have enjoyed in the past.

Senator DORGAN. Well, I share the view that if we do nothing, all of those plans that are on the drawing boards at this point for new buildings and buildings partially under construction, I assume there are consequences for all of that activity, and the result would be a real depressing effect on the economy, an economy that is already struggling mightily, in my judgment one that requires a stimulus package now. This would be exactly the opposite influence on the economy at exactly the worst possible moment.

But I was getting to a different point. Will there be at some point a market evaluation of the pricing of this so that there comes a time when we do something that intervenes and then it is handed off to the market system that prices what is the risk, and how do we price the risk with respect to these activities?

Secretary O'NEILL. We are anticipating that as we go through next year we will begin to gather some experience, and as we go through the next 3 years we will gather a considerable amount of experience, and the insurance industry and the private sector will figure out how to deal with this problem, and honestly, if we did not think we were headed towards this cliff effect we would not be here at all, because many of us are from the private sector, and believe that the private sector can work out most problems. We do not think the private sector is going to come to a conclusion that works very well for our economy because of the uncertainty of dealing with terrorist risks.

Senator DORGAN. Well, Mr. Secretary, I think your testimony is helpful to us, and I do think we have to take action. I would agree with many of my colleagues saying that I do not think we ought to be participating in the first dollar of loss. I think that ideas that have been developed around an approach that would create a safe haven beyond which we would participate makes the most sense.

Having taught some economics in college, I really believe the market system works well, but it occasionally does not work at all, and I am always amused that, depending upon the hearing you are involved with and whose interests are affected, you hear people say the market system ought to be relied upon, and it is always the bigger interest in which when the market system fails, people say, we have got to get involved, but somehow the little folks do not get so much help.

I do think your testimony is helpful to our committee and to our congress, and I think we have to move. I do not think we can possibly go to the end of this year and do nothing, because I worry that this economy is in much more trouble than most people understand. I think September 11 put a hole in the belly of this economy that was already struggling in a way that most of us do not quite fathom, and so we must not only try to give it lift, we must avoid doing things that provide a depressing impact on the economy, and doing nothing with respect to this issue in my judgment would be almost irresponsible, so the question is not whether, it is how, and I am anxious to work with you, as are my colleagues, to find a way to solve this problem.

Mr. Secretary, thank you.

The CHAIRMAN. Thank you. Senator Fitzgerald, and this is the last one. I know the Secretary has been trying to get away, and you have been very gracious with your time. Thank you.

Senator FITZGERALD. Mr. Secretary, I want to congratulate you. I have been following closely your activities in the administration since September 11, and I think you have been a real strong voice for the taxpayers. I know you were advocating restraint in the airline bailout, and I think more so than many on Capitol Hill, and even elsewhere in the administration, and so I want to thank you.

I actually think that you may be right in your proposal providing the first dollars as opposed to the Banking Committee's approach, and I will tell you why I think that. In the private sector, I was General Counsel for a bank holding company, and I understand fully what happens if a borrower cannot have insurance. That is immediate grounds for foreclosure by the bank. It is malpractice for a banking attorney at a loan closing not to get evidence of paid-up real estate taxes and a paid-up insurance binder showing the lender as the mortgage loss payee.

If the owner of the World Trade Center had some insurance, those insurance proceeds are not going to be paid to him, they are going to be paid to whoever is his lender; and, in fact, his lender may be an insurance company in this case, as most tall buildings are financed by life insurance companies, and I wonder—I understand the concern everybody has with the government providing the first dollars, but let us consider the example of the Sears Tower in Chicago, the world's tallest building, actually taller than the Petronis Towers, if you do not count antennas, and it is taller than the World Trade Center was by a little bit.

If there is a deductible for the insurance companies, who is going to provide a policy for that building? Am I right in that assessment?

Secretary O'NEILL. You are absolutely right.

Senator FITZGERALD. One of your objectives must be to allow people who own commercial buildings—who want to build new commercial buildings—to be able to get insurance. The deductible approach will not solve that problem as far as I can tell, at least not on tall buildings.

Secretary O'NEILL. Well, again, we can rely on some experience, and you all I am sure have had your own automobile insurance, and you know how automobile insurance works. If you are over 25 years old and you are married and you have three children and you do not drink and smoke, you can get what is called a preferred premium because you are a low risk.

If, on the other hand, you are 16 years old and you do all those other things, then you are an assigned risk, and your policy premium may be three or four or ten times bigger than it is for your parents, and the same goes for—let us use your example, high rise buildings. There is going to be, there has always been, and there will be, we think, an assigned risk pool for the obvious targets of terrorist acts, and the essential question is, how much of a deductible can the industry deal with in going to people that are going to be in the assigned risk pool and charge them a premium that discharges the cost exposure that an insurance company is accepting and still is affordable from the point of view of an owner or a borrower?

That is the essential issue, and it is why we have taken this 80/20 approach, because we think the reinsurance process of mutualizing risk can deal with $4 billion. As the numbers mount, it becomes more problematic whether the people in the assigned risk pool and even the people in the non-assigned risk pool are going to be able to pay the premiums that give them access to financial markets. That is the unknown.

Senator FITZGERALD. My question would be, why not adopt something like the riot risk concerns pool that we started in the sixties? I know you want to have the government involvement here be very temporary, but I question our ability to exit in 3 years for the very reason that most commercial real estate is financed on a very long-term basis. It will not be enough for somebody to line up a construction loan to build a building if no one is willing to give him a 30-year mortgage at the end of the construction period. If we do not have the insurance problem solved on a long-term basis, I do not know that we are going to solve the inhibitions that the current climate is creating in the construction industry and in the commercial office building industry.

Secretary O'NEILL. Again, a couple of things from experience. It is the general practice to have a 1-year cancellation provision in property and casualty insurance, and so I think having a 1-year duration is not a problem, and it is not unusual to have construction-only insurance provisions, so I think with what we are proposing we can gain some experience and hopefully not have to do something that becomes a more permanent engagement of the federal government in regulating and directing the U.S. insurance industry, but I think none of us know the longer-term answers to these issues which you very appropriately raise, and it really cries out for a year's worth of experience, and as best we can, a couple of years worth of design parameters, which is what we have suggested for year 2 and year 3, and if I were writing this legislation—and I have said this to the other committee—I would put in a provision that says in 15 months we want you to come back. We want to know how much premiums were collected, how much insurance face value was written, what are the problems that have developed under this process, and how can we improve this so that it is beneficial to the American economy.

Senator DORGAN. (presiding) Mr. Secretary, thank you very much for your appearance today. We appreciate it.

Secretary O'NEILL. Thank you all very much.

Senator DORGAN. While the Secretary departs, we would like to announce we will have both panel II and III come to the dais together. We have three witnesses in the second panel and four witnesses in the third, and I would like to ask if we could get a couple of additional chairs at the table so we could have all seven witnesses come up.

We will ask Mr. David Keating, senior counsel, National Taxpayers Union to come forward, Ms. Diane Koken, Commissioner of Insurance for the Commonwealth of Pennsylvania, Mr. David Moss, associate professor, Harvard Building School, Mr. Phillip Hawkins, chief operating officer, CarrAmerica Realty, Mr. Franklin Nutter, president, Reinsurance Association of America, Mr. Travis Plunkett, legislative director for the Consumer Federation of America, and Mr. Robert Vagley, president of the American Insurance Association.

Senator DORGAN. We thank all of you for being here with us today, and because of the hour, late in the afternoon, we are going to combine the panels. We would take them in the order that I have announced them. I believe first will be Mr. David Keating, senior counsel, National Taxpayers Union.

STATEMENT OF MR. DAVID KEATING, SENIOR COUNSELOR, NATIONAL TAXPAYERS UNION

Mr. KEATING. Thank you, Mr. Chairman, members of the committee for holding this hearing and for your interest in offering some protection not only to people operating businesses and homes across the country, but the American taxpayer. We have some very serious concerns in opposition to the administration's proposal as it was presented, as well as the industry proposal, although that seems to be on the back burner at this time.

We believe that insurance companies do have to pay if there is going to be a federal reinsurance program. They need to pay, otherwise they will compete by giving the coverage away to their clients, and we think this creates problems, not only moral hazards for the insurance concepts, but security hazards.

We also believe that insurers will have little or no incentive to underwrite individual risks with any caution to avoid concentration risks or to help clients reduce their own risks. They will assume more risk for the government than they ever would have if their own money were at risk. We think it is very important that if the congress moves forward on a program here to limit the government's total liabilities, set firm limits per policy, clearly define terrorism, and limit the government's exposure to certain types of losses such as business interruption.

My testimony outlines a number of principles that I hope Congress will abide by if it decides to move forward with a program. One is that any federal capacity offered should offer the maximum amount of economic benefit to the Nation, as well as to injured parties at the lowest possible cost to the taxpayer.

Another important principle is that legislation must not erode strong incentives for wise underwriting and insurance company management of risk. In other words, we do not want to take away incentives for insurance companies to work with their clients to minimize losses, and that means proper security and proper escape contingency plans. This is not only important to safeguard against the risk of loss of property, but the loss of human life.

As I said earlier, we also think that it is crucial that if federal reinsurance capacity is offered, then there should be a payment for the use of this capital of the federal government and the assumption of risk.

We also believe that federal coverage should not insure against all industry terror losses, 1) because of the incentives that would be taken away to increased security, but we also think it is important that insurance companies properly monitor claims administration. It is very easy to make people happy when you have no money at stake, or very little. If you are paying out a claim of a dollar, and you only pay 10 cents, there is not an incentive to watch to make sure those claims are being properly administered.

We also support the concept of making the capacity temporary. We believe market mechanisms should be used to the extent possible, and we should encourage the reentry of private reinsurance at high levels at the earliest possible date.

I was quite disturbed to hear Secretary O'Neill say earlier that some consideration was being given to removing the cap. We think it is very important that the Federal Government's total exposure be capped. Whether it is $100 billion, or $60 billion, or some cap, there needs to be a cap. We cannot write a federal entitlement program to insure against unlimited losses. If we are going to be fighting a war, we need to make sure the federal government has the fiscal flexibility to win that war, and you cannot do that if you take unlimited risk for everything, so it is very important to keep a cap on the total amount covered.

We also believe that there needs to be some mediation panel or some efficient way of solving disputes about claims. We do not want the federal government and the taxpayer's money wrapped up in paying a lot of unnecessary litigation costs and dragging out claims over many years.

We also believe there needs to be a clear definition of what is a terror loss and what losses are covered.

Now, to turn my attention to the administration's proposal, it does have some sensible provisions of capping federal liability—that is important—providing for cost-sharing, although the cost shares are too high for the government, and it does have a sunset provision. That is good.

I do want to point out that many things are sunsetted in Washington, and the sun always seems to rise once again, and we believe that if you give away federal reinsurance, which the administration is proposing to do, people are going to say, I love getting free things, let's have more of it, so even though there is a sunset after 3 years, the sun may well rise again.

As far as the administration's plan goes, there are six points we would like to make about how it can be improved.

We think each individual company should have a retention amount, or deductible.

We think there should be a payment for the federal reinsurance. We suggest 1 percent of each company's insured volume less the retention amount.

We think reinsurance should not pay more than 80 percent of all claims over the retention amount, and diminishing amount in the outyears.

We also think it is important that the tax penalty against reserving for terror risks should be repealed for all insurance companies. This would help increase private sector capacity.

I see my time is up, so I will just end right here. Our testimony, our written statement also has a suggestion for an alternative facility that would allow the private sector to take as much of the risk as possible as quickly as possible, and give not only the federal government but the individual insurance companies real incentives to manage these claims properly, to manage security risk properly, and to get out of the business as quickly as possible.

Thank you very much.

[The statement of Mr. Keating follows:]

PREPARED STATEMENT OF DAVID L. KEATING, SENIOR COUNSELOR, NATIONAL TAXPAYERS UNION

Mr. Chairman, and members of the Committee, thank you for the opportunity to present our views on proposals for terror reinsurance. The 335,000-member National Taxpayers Union strongly opposes the proposals offered by the insurance industry and the Administration, both of which would violate key principles of sound insurance policymaking. These flaws would put lives and property in danger and expose taxpayers to unnecessary losses.

Congress should move cautiously as precedents may be created for Congressional responses to other large losses and major insurance industry difficulties.

Unless insurance companies have to pay—and pay a lot—for Federal reinsurance, they will compete by giving the coverage away to clients. This creates moral and security hazards. Second—and this is very important—they will have no incentive to underwrite individual risks with any caution, to avoid concentration risks or to help their clients reduce their risks. They will assume more risk for the government than they ever would have if their own money were at risk.

It is essential to limit the government's total liabilities, set firm limits per policy, clearly define terrorism and limit the government's exposure to certain types of loss (*e.g.*, business interruption). Otherwise, we could be paying companies not to be going back to work for years. Of course, the insurers should have to pay enough of the claims, a minimum of 20 percent in the first year, to carefully monitor claims administration.

Too often legislation is passed as a quick response to a problem without addressing fundamental flaws in public policy. During our work over the last six years studying proposed legislation and public policy regarding natural disasters, we have found that a number of Federal and state laws and regulations greatly hamper the ability of the private sector to provide insurance for catastrophes.

Perhaps the most important impediment to affordable insurance against manmade or natural catastrophes is the Federal tax law, which contains a huge implicit tax penalty on businesses and homeowners who attempt to purchase such insurance. These same laws prevent insurance companies from deducting an amount equal to the risk of catastrophic natural disasters or terror attacks; amounts that we consider legitimate business expenses. We hope this problem will be corrected and urge the Committee to use the Policyholder Disaster Protection Act (HR 785), by Representatives Foley and Matsui, as a starting point.

It is not clear to us whether a Federal terror reinsurance program is needed at this time. Certainly it is completely unacceptable to enact a program that would increase risks to lives, property and federal finances.

Insurers are not claiming they are in trouble, only that the market *may* fail to respond to higher pricing with more capacity. That's dubious at best and there's a good case to be made that we ought to wait and see what happens in the market. Even if terrorism is excluded from some policies, life and business will certainly go on.

Since the Sept. 11 attacks, property and casualty insurers' stocks have significantly outperformed the S&P 500, and the stocks are up, not down. Insurance stocks' performance shows a great deal about market experts' view of the industry's future claims-paying ability, future risk, and the opportunities associated with expected higher pricing. It also shows—along with the new company announcements—that the capital markets have in no way restricted the industry's ability to raise capital and take on additional risk.

If Congress enacts such a reinsurance program, we strongly urge you to be guided by the following principles.

1. *Any Federal capacity should offer the maximum amount of economic benefit to the nation as well as injured parties at the lowest possible cost to the taxpayer.*

2. *Legislation must not erode strong incentives for wise underwriting and insurance company management of risks (e.g., proper security and escape contingency plans).* If no reinsurance is available, then the insurance industry will continue to cover claims until their current policies expire or a time the current policy allows for modification of the coverage. Until then, the insurance companies have an extremely high incentive to help their clients take sensible steps to reduce their risk of terrorism loss. Likewise, if a business finds it cannot insure for terror risks when its policy expires, it too will take much more vigilant steps to secure its property, customers and employees. A blank federal reinsurance check would eliminate a very important incentive to increase security.

3. *If Federal reinsurance capacity is offered, then there should be payment for the use of that capital and assumption of risk.* Any plan that fails to collect premiums is a giveaway that will increase losses from any future attacks since it would undermine insurer incentives to boost security and create effective disaster control and reaction plans. It would be irresponsible to discourage effective safeguards that can reduce the number of lives and amount of property that could be lost from a terror attack. While no one knows how to price this risk since the market is not offering it now, the government should attempt to price it at a level that would likely be charged by the private sector after it emerges from this market disruption. The Treasury should use very conservative assumptions in pricing for that risk so that the private sector can retake this market as soon as possible.

4. *Federal coverage should certainly not insure against all industry terror losses.* Coverage of the first dollar of losses is both unnecessary and unwise because this too will erode incentives to increase security. Lower levels of financial risk should remain in the private sector, which will attempt to price the insurance for the limited risk. Those price signals will provide important pricing information to the government for the use of its capacity. If the government provides coverage, we strongly recommend restricting coverage to property loss and workers' compensation only. If insureds also want business interruption coverage, they can go to the private sector for supplemental coverage.

5. *Federal reinsurance capacity should be temporary, maximize the use of market mechanisms and encourage the reentry of private reinsurance at higher levels at the earliest possible date.* We must rigorously avoid any establishment of a permanent entity. Insurance is available for many other large and highly uncertain risks and terror insurance will be more efficiently administered and priced by the private sector in the long run. It is too easy to make a mistake in haste, which could prove impossible politically to fix later.

6. *Legislation must contain strong incentives to pay only valid claims.* The Federal government's co-payment of claims should never exceed 80 percent, and 70 percent or less would be preferable. It is easy for insurance companies to keep customers happy if they have little or no financial incentive to monitor claims for fraud and overpayments.

7. *The federal government's exposure must be capped to preserve America's national security options.* The Federal government must not insure against unlimited terror or war risks. In the event of a war or a terror attack with weapons of mass destruction, the losses would be far more serious than those experienced in the September 11th attacks. The government needs to limit its liability so that it can preserve the fiscal flexibility needed to fight a war.

8. *Incentives should be created to get the federal government out of this business and reduce its role to covering a higher layer of loss as early as possible.*

9. *A mediation panel is needed to quickly pay and settle claims for terror losses in a fair and inexpensive way.* However undesirable it may be to spend taxpayer monies on terrorism losses of property, it will be completely

unacceptable to pay large amounts to the trial bar in the aftermath of an event, and further slow the process of getting funds into the hands of rightful recipients. Any non-productive activity such as litigation, which slows the process of pricing the event, will lead to more uncertainty in repricing insurance for future events and will add to the ultimate cost of such events. Such a variation was included in the airline industry bailout. If people do not wish to waive their rights to sue, then they should purchase their own terrorism coverage, unsubsidized by the government.

10. *Legislation should contain a clear definition of what is a terror loss, and all other losses should be excluded from coverage.* The formulation of coverage will need to be quite specific or there will be lots of opportunities for financial mischief at taxpayers' expense. This definition would then need to be met on any private industry claim payment, prior to allowing either the customer or the insurance company to present the balance of the claim to the government. If this definition is not clear or not rigorously applied, there will be endless disputes. We strongly believe that any program should be limited to property coverage, where losses are easier to verify.

11. *Federal law should override any state terror insurance regulations until the Federal capacity has disappeared.*

The Administration Proposal

The proposal is a public-private sector program. In 2002, the government would absorb 80 percent of the first $20 billion of insured losses resulting from terrorism, and 90 percent of insured losses above $20 billion.

In 2003, the private sector would handle the first $10 billion of loss. Losses between $10 billion and $20 billion would be shared, with the government paying 50 percent and the private sector paying 50 percent. After losses exceed $20 billion, the government would cover 90 percent of losses, and the private sector would cover 10 percent.

In 2004, the private sector would cover the first $20 billion in losses. Between $20 billion and $40 billion of losses, the government and private sector would each cover 50 percent of the losses. At above $40 billion in losses, the government would pay 90 percent of losses.

Overall liability would be capped at $100 billion.

The Administration plan has some sensible provisions. We support the provisions that cap Federal liability, provide for cost sharing (though the shares are too high for the government) and eliminate the program after three years.

Still there are many serious problems with the Administration proposal.

1. *If Federal reinsurance capacity is offered, then there should be payment for the use of that capital and assumption of risk.* Any plan that fails to collect premiums is a giveaway that will increase losses from any future attacks since it would undermine insurer incentives to boost security and create effective disaster control and reaction plans.

2. *Federal coverage should certainly not insure against all industry terror losses.* Coverage of the first dollar of losses is both unnecessary and unwise because this too will erode incentives to increase security and monitor claims for fraud and overpayments. Coverage of the first dollar of losses for all insurance companies would also lead to an unnecessary increase in Federal bureaucracy, costs, and insurance waste. It is hard to find any consumer or business insurance policies that do not have some form of a deductible, and Federal terror reinsurance shouldn't eliminate this sound principle of insurance.

3. *Legislation must contain strong incentives to pay only valid claims.* The Federal government's co-payment of claims should never exceed 80 percent. The co-payment by the insurance companies must be substantial in order to guard against excessive claims payments.

4. *The plan should clearly define coverage, and should not cover risks that are harder to verify such as business interruption and liability insurance.*

We should note that the "industry" doesn't insure anything; individual companies do, and these companies vary considerably in their capabilities and capacity. It isn't apparent how the Administration's plan would distribute the losses around the industry. Individual companies write individual risks that will incur discreet losses (some of which might be covered, some not under normal policy conditions), then claim payments are made as negotiated with each individual client. Risks and losses are not distributed proportionately around the market, as will be seen when the cost of September 11 is tallied.

The New York Times reported Oct. 22 that Berkshire Hathaway chief executive Warren Buffett said, "I think there is nothing wrong with having the industry lose a lot of money if something like [a terror attack] happens. We just have to keep it within the ability of the industry to pay. The industry can pay for a $10 billion loss. It can't price for a $500 billion loss."

Lower levels of exposure should remain in the private sector, which will price the insurance for the limited exposures. Those price signals will provide important pricing information to the government for its reinsurance capacity.

Improving the Administration Proposal

The Administration proposal can be greatly improved with some key modifications. Clearly, the Federal government must charge for its reinsurance capacity and the coverage should kick in at higher levels.

In addition to the provisions contained in the Administration plan, these key provisions are needed:

1. Each individual company should have a retention amount (or deductible) for terror claims.
2. We recommend making the payment for the Federal reinsurance equal to one percent of each company's insured volume less the retention amount.
3. The reinsurance would pay 80 percent of all claims over the retention amount in the first year, and diminishing amounts in the second and third years.
4. To help build capacity in the private sector, the tax penalty against reserving for terror risks would be repealed for all insurance companies. This provision could be drafted by using the Policyholder Disaster Protection Act (HR 785), by Representatives Foley and Matsui, as a starting point. The phase-in provisions in this bill should be deleted.
5. The coverage should be clearly defined to cover only actual commercial property losses and workers' compensation.
6. A mediation panel is needed to quickly pay and settle claims for terror losses in a fair and inexpensive way.

While it may seem like a good idea for the Federal government to stay out of pricing, we must not lose sight of the fact that the Federal government is offering $88 billion in reserves against terror losses. It should certainly charge some reasonable amount for that risk.

If the insurance companies are covering only 12 percent of losses, then they should be receiving, on average, 12 percent of the associated premium. Since there is no traditional way to estimate or annualize losses, there probably should be a nominal "load" established to be added to every dollar of non-terrorism premium.

We strongly recommend that the first year of the program also require that the private sector cover at least the first $10 billion of losses. After that amount the government should cover no more than 80 percent of additional losses.

In 2003, the private sector should cover the first $15 billion of losses. Between $15 billion and $25 billion, the private sector should cover 50 percent of losses, and between $25 billion and $100 billion, the government would cover 70 percent of additional losses.

In 2004, the private sector should cover the first $25 billion of losses. Between $25 billion and $100 billion, the private sector should cover 50 percent of losses.

A Plan for a Public and Private Terrorism Facility, with Increasing Share Being Owned by The Private Sector at Higher Levels of Capacity

All of the proposed Federal terrorism reinsurance plans offered to date violate key principles of sound insurance policymaking. These flaws would put lives and property in danger and expose taxpayers to unnecessary losses.

If Congress concludes it must do something to provide capacity and maintain insurance for terror risks, there is a better way to set up a terrorism facility. Our suggestion is an approach that would involve the industry financially and operationally while creating incentives to properly price and manage risks. The strength of this proposal is that it creates extremely powerful incentives for the facility to operate efficiently, minimize risks to lives and property and carefully pay claims.

Equally important, the industry and government have immensely powerful financial incentives to disband the facility after three years. A wonderful bonus of the dissolution would be a huge improvement in the capacity of the industry to pay for man-made or natural mega-catastrophes.

This facility allows the Federal backstop to constantly move up, farther from the risk as time goes on, with the Federal backstop eventually being eliminated entirely as a result of accumulating funds in the facility.

This facility was designed to last for three years, but could easily work for just one year or two years.

We welcome comments and suggested improvements to this proposal.

1. Each company would invest capital to prime the facility, with an initial investment of 2 percent of the previous year's annualized premium charges. This would give the facility about $6 billion of capital at its launch, and would serve to start the operation with no outlay of Federal funds.

2. The total capacity and liability of the facility would equal $100 billion, with the Federal Government providing the difference between the facility's capital and total liability. For example, after one year (if no losses occurred and ignoring investment income) the facility would have $36 billion, with Federal backstop loan availability of $64 billion.

3. If a Federal backstop loan is triggered, the Government would be repaid over a 20-year period at the then-prevailing interest rate for 20-year borrowings by an S&P rated AA financial institution.

4. The facility would be permitted to build reserves for terror risks on a tax-deferred basis.

5. The facility would cover only real and personal property loss and workers' compensation arising from a formally declared event and only for those losses defined in the facility's charter.

6. Each company would have a retention equal to 20 percent of its written premium as a self-insured loss, to be funded by it from its general revenue and investments. Individual companies would be free to reinsure this amount commercially if possible.

7. After the individual company retention, the facility would pay 80 percent of remaining losses, which would be pro-rated if total losses exceed $100 billion per year.

8. Terror losses eligible to be paid by the facility and the Federal government would be specifically declared and certified by the Secretary of the Treasury, and claims would be paid to/through individual companies after they had presented evidence of payment of their 20 percent share of any declared loss.

9. Quarterly, each company would collect from its customers and remit an amount equal to 10 percent of their gross written premium collections to the facility. These additional premiums would carry no agent or broker commissions and the insurers would make no administrative charge for collecting and remitting these funds. The premiums so collected would be specifically designated as funding the national terrorism facility, and insurers would be expressly and legally prohibited from charging customers any other premiums related to the coverage provided by the national facility. Absent any major loss after one year, this facility would have accumulated about $30 billion in added capital plus investment earnings of approximately $750 million. Investments could be limited to US government obligations. If no losses occurred, the facility would have private funding of $100 billion in less than 3.3 years.

10. To allow for coordination between companies to participate in the facility and to coordinate with each other to manage the terror risk, participating companies and the facility itself would receive an exemption from anti-trust laws as applicable to these specific activities.

11. State regulations regarding rates and coverages for terror risk would be preempted until the Federal backstop capacity is no longer in place.

12. Senior management's compensation would include a substantial bonus if Federal risk is reduced and other management goals are met. The management goals would include (other suggestions welcomed):

- Minimizing Federal exposure through securitizing risk through issuing catastrophe bonds or buying reinsurance.
- Efficient operations.
- Timely payment of claims.
- Accurate and fair claims administration.

13. To avoid any potential conflicts of interest, a Supervisory Board would be composed of the Treasury and industry officials with consumer and taxpayer representatives. The chairman and majority control of the Board would remain with Treasury officials until the industry has contributed $75 billion in capital and the facility had accumulated that much capital. At that time, the chairmanship and control of the board would switch to industry representatives.

14. The facility must at all times maintain an independent risk management function for controlling risk assessment, risk management, pricing, money management and claims assessments. It would report to management and the Board.

15. A mediation panel would quickly resolve any disputed claims for terror losses in a fair and inexpensive way. This would ensure that victims would receive quick payment of disputed claims and minimize non-productive litigation. Quick and fair resolution will lead to more certainty in pricing insurance for future events and will therefore both reduce the ultimate cost of such events and allow the private sector to more quickly reenter the market.

16. If losses were minor, the facility would disband after three years. If the facility disbands, then its capital (including accumulated investment income), after payment of Federal income taxes at the then-prevailing corporate tax rate, would be distributed to each company according to the amount invested. Using this formula, if the facility had $100 billion in capital for distribution, the Government would receive approximately $35 billion prior to the return of the funds to the contributing insurers. The after-tax capital would then be distributed to the insurance companies with a requirement that it be placed in a special tax-deferred reserve fund at each company. These reserves could only be used to pay for man-made or natural mega-catastrophe losses in a manner similar to the provisions of the Policyholder Disaster Protection Act (HR 785), by Representatives Foley and Matsui.

A facility of this type would require a small number of very capable people to operate; probably outsourcing most labor and computer intensive functions so as to keep fixed overhead at a minimum. All administrative and operating expenses could be paid using a very small percentage of the accumulated funds.

At a minimum, this new facility should be the provider of terrorism coverage for all commercial enterprises and subject to mandatory participation by all property and casualty companies. Carriers could provide coverage themselves for personal lines risks or for risks outside the precise coverage definition approved by Treasury if they want to, (perhaps even take reserves offshore,) but they would still need to pay for this facility if they conduct any business in the United States.

The Insurance Industry Proposal

We are strongly opposed to the industry bill as presented in its most recent draft, which is riddled with both short and long-term flaws. It is completely contrary to at least principles 1–10 listed above on pages 2–4.

The proposal appears to create an unlimited liability for the Federal government for terror risks. The legislation also covers an unclear amount of war risks. As noted previously, the Federal government must have complete flexibility during war because the most important function of our government is to defend the country. We cannot and must not create an entitlement program to insure against all terror or war risks, which may cripple the financial capacity of the government to win the war.

This proposal initially offers no payment to the Federal government for its reinsurance capacity, and it is quite possible that no payment would ever be forthcoming. We are strongly opposed to any such giveaway. Just because it is difficult to properly charge for the risk doesn't mean that nothing should be charged.

The pool concept is fundamentally flawed, and there are better alternatives. It allows companies to be looser in their underwriting and increases moral hazard problems compared to alternatives. Companies could shift risk in an undetectable manner to the pool.

Another key concern is that the proposal would set up a permanent bureaucracy that would greatly expand its mission over time, concentrating risk and displacing a healthy reinsurance market.

This facility would have enormous advantages that no other firm could match, including tax-free reserving, explicit access to Federal credit and a location in one of the least-regulated states in the country. At the end of its "life" there is to be a report on the state of capacity in the industry, not just for terror, but for other large risks currently handled by the private sector such as natural disasters.

We understand that the proposal has a sunset clause, but are not reassured. Once federal programs start, they rarely disappear, and this entity will have powerful allies who will likely seek to dump their other least attractive risks on the taxpayer. Important sectors of the industry have been trying for years to push legislation through the Congress to set up a natural disaster insurance corporation, and this entity could well take on that role as it is about to supposedly expire.

The inherent advantages of the proposed "Homeland" insurance entity would make it almost impossible for the private sector to move back into the business of insuring against terror risks as it could not compete against Homeland's awesome advantages in amassing tax-free reserves and accessing Federal credit.

Conclusion

Proposals for Federal insurance for terror and war risks are both politically and economically risky and should be subjected to extensive examination and comment before being enacted into law. We strongly urge the Committee to remember that even the best-intentioned programs can have budget-busting consequences. In this case, a poorly designed program would also place more lives at risk and conceivably harm the financial ability of the government to defend the country. Congress must move carefully in this highly complex area to ensure that it does not create a fiscal disaster, unwisely interfere with private markets or violate sound insurance principles.

Senator DORGAN. Mr. Keating, thank you for your testimony. Thank you for being here.

Next, we will hear from Ms. Diane Koken, Commissioner of Insurance for the Commonwealth of Pennsylvania. Ms. Koken.

STATEMENT OF MS. DIANE KOKEN, COMMISSIONER OF INSURANCE FOR THE COMMONWEALTH OF PENNSYLVANIA, NATIONAL ASSOCIATION OF INSURANCE COMMISSIONERS

Ms. KOKEN. Thank you very much. In addition to being Commissioner of Insurance in Pennsylvania, I am also chair of the Northeast Zone of NAIC, and I am here today to testify on behalf of the National Association of Insurance Commissioners.

I would like to make three basic points. First, the NAIC and its members believe there is presently a need for the federal government, working with the state regulatory system, to provide appropriate financial backup to the private insurance market in order to assure that our nation's economy does not falter due to a lack of insurance coverage for terrorism.

Although the NAIC has not endorsed a specific proposal for federal assistance at this time, we have adopted a set of 19 guiding principles that we believe form the basis for any successful federal program.

Second, we believe federal assistance should be a relatively short-term solution to stabilize the commercial marketplace while it regains the risk assessment and pricing equilibrium needed for private insurers to underwrite terrorism exposures. Thus, any federal terrorism program should be limited in scope and duration, and should also include a national definition of terrorism.

Third, a federal assistance program should maximize the use of market forces to add efficiency and reduce the risk of losses from terrorism and the potential cost to federal taxpayers.

The United States insurance system remains fundamentally sound. Let me start by saying the NAIC does believe the insurance industry is well-capitalized and financially able to withstand the pressures created by the terror attack on September 11. The United States insurance industry has a $1 trillion business, with assets of more than $3 trillion. Preliminary loss estimates of $30 billion to $40 billion represent just 3 to 4 percent of the premiums written in 2000.

As regulators, my colleagues and I will continue monitoring the process on behalf of consumers to make sure that insurance promises are kept. To do our job, we are backed by an impressive array of human and technical resources, including the NAIC and 51 insurance departments that collectively employ more than 10,000 people. We would urge congress to structure any federal assistance program to take full advantage of the existing state regulatory system. We have the mechanisms in place to monitor insurers' solvency and handle claims payment issues.

Congress should not disrupt the power of private market competition. There are three important market factors for congress to keep in mind. First, following the September 11 attacks, government and commercial facilities across America have added security measures to help prevent acts of terrorism and limit potential damages. As commercial risk managers review these new precautions, it seems likely that they will become more inclined to offer terrorism insurance because the possibility and extent of potential insured losses occurring will be greatly reduced.

At that point, we expect market forces will start working to fill the gap by making terrorism insurance available through private industry. The NAIC recommends that congress build in strong incentives for insurers or companies receiving federal assistance to implement and maintain effective risk management measures to prevent acts of terrorism from occurring.

Second, the private market instills policyholder discipline to avoid insurance claims through the concept of co-insurance. Co-insurance means that policyholders are liable to pay part of any losses covered by insurance before expecting a recovery from an insurer. This concept is commonly understood by everyone owning a car or a home who agrees to bear a cost of a deductible.

Third, the scope and duration of any federal assistance program will itself become a factor in the private insurance market. The NAIC urges you to keep in mind the federal government policy regarding terrorism insurance assistance will not occur in a vacuum. The extent of the federal influence on private market insurance products can be expected to be directly commensurate with the size, details, and length of the federal assistance program. state actions are not driving the market demand for terrorism insurance.

The NAIC and its members have recently been asked to explain how requirements of state law impact the market demand for terrorism insurance. Many people in congress think that states require private businesses to carry insurance against terrorism and that failure of the private insurance market to offer terrorism coverage will result in violating state laws and regulations. This is a misunderstanding of what state laws require and what state insurance regulators do. To our knowledge, no state currently requires that business entities maintain insurance against acts of terrorism. It is important to understand that state insurance regulators do not normally get involved in the details of property casualty insurance policies for large, sophisticated business operations. These are considered to be the product of free market negotiations among sophisticated insurance underwriters, brokers, and professional corporate risk managers who rely upon the traditional powers of buyers and sellers to bargain for the best deal they can get.

The NAIC and state regulators believe the insurance industry remains strong, and that it retains tremendous resiliency to recover from the September 11 attacks and adjust its business practices to new conditions in the marketplace. We are working together to help assure that any glitches which occur do not disrupt the process of getting people's lives back in order and America's business back to work. The NAIC and its members plan to work closely with congress and fellow regulators so that the needs of the individual Americans and the nation's economy are met in a timely way.

Thank you very much.

[The statement of Ms. Koken follows:]

PREPARED STATEMENT OF DIANE KOKEN, COMMISSIONER OF INSURANCE FOR THE COMMONWEALTH OF PENNSYLVANIA, NATIONAL ASSOCIATION OF INSURANCE COMMISSIONERS

Introduction

My name is Diane Koken. I am the Commissioner of Insurance for the Commonwealth of Pennsylvania, and I also serve as chair of the National Association of Insurance Commissioners' (NAIC) Northeast Zone comprising 10 states and the District of Columbia. Speaking for myself and fellow members of the NAIC, we appreciate the opportunity to testify regarding the potential role of the federal government in making sure that insurance against acts of terrorism remains available to American consumers and businesses.

Today, I want to make three basic points:

- First, NAIC and its members believe there is presently a need for the federal government, working with the state regulatory system, to provide appropriate financial back-up to the private insurance market in order to assure that our nation's economy does not falter due to a lack of insurance coverage for terrorism. Although NAIC has not endorsed a specific proposal for federal assistance at this time, we have adopted a set of 19 guiding principles that we believe should form the basis of any successful federal program. A copy of the NAIC's guiding principles is attached at the end of my testimony.
- Second, we believe federal assistance should be a relatively short-term solution to stabilize the commercial marketplace while it regains the risk assessment and pricing equilibrium needed for private insurers to underwrite terrorism exposures. Thus, any federal terrorism insurance program should be limited in scope and duration.
- Third, a federal assistance program should maximize the use of market forces to add efficiency and reduce the risk of losses from terrorism and the potential costs to federal taxpayers.

The United States Insurance System Remains Fundamentally Sound

Let me start by saying that NAIC believes the insurance industry is well-capitalized and financially able to withstand the pressures created by the September 11th terrorist attacks, despite losses projected to exceed $30 billion. The United States insurance industry is a $1 trillion business with assets of more than $3 trillion. Preliminary loss estimates of $30 billion to $40 billion represent just 3 to 4 percent of the premiums written in 2000.

America's insurance companies have time and again shown their ability to respond to huge disasters and successfully recover. Adjusted for inflation, Hurricane Andrew in 1992 caused $19.7 billion in insured losses, and California's Northridge Earthquake in 1994 cost $16.3 billion in insured losses. As with previous disasters, we believe insurers affected by the recent terrorist attacks will be able to pay their projected claims, as they themselves have said.

Insurance is the sale of a promise to pay claims when losses occur. As regulators, my colleagues and I will continue monitoring the process to make sure that insurance promises are kept. To do our job, we are backed by an impressive array of human and technical resources, including the NAIC and fifty-one state insurance departments that collectively employ more than 10,400 people and spend $910 million annually on insurance supervision. In addition, at this time state insurance guaranty funds have the capacity to provide up to $10 billion to compensate American consumers in the event of insurer insolvencies.

We would urge Congress to structure any federal assistance program to take full advantage of the existing state regulatory system. We have the mechanisms in place to monitor insurer solvency and handle claims payment issues.

Congress Should Not Disrupt the Power of Private Market Competition

The international commercial property/casualty insurance market is very powerful, dynamic, and competitive. As a free market, it responds to new information quickly, and sometimes with great volatility. Like the stock exchanges, insurance market participants often react in unison to reach the same conclusion at the same time with regard to what products are viable and profitable, meaning that the price and availability of specific products will rise and fall in conjunction with the industry's collective willingness to sell them. Substantially negative information, such as the September 11th terrorist attacks, can disrupt the entire market until new information becomes available that makes insuring terrorist risks acceptable.

Given sufficient time to adjust, however, the commercial insurance market has found ways in the past to assess and insure extremely large and difficult risks that were initially considered uninsurable. During the 1980's and 1990's, the insurance industry weathered enormous financial losses from asbestos, medical malpractice, and environmental pollution claims against corporate policyholders that were not foreseen by insurers. In those instances, insurers said they had not reasonably expected to be held responsible for such colossal claims, and therefore had not collected sufficient premiums or established sufficient loss reserves to cover them.

In the short term, the insurance market responded to huge environmental exposures with policy cancellations, coverage limitations, exclusions, and increased prices, as is being threatened now with regard to terrorism risk coverage. In the longer term, coverage for these risks became available through a combination of aggressive risk management, self-insurance, captive insurance pools, other alternative risk-sharing mechanisms, and renewed interest by commercial insurers as they gained confidence in their abilities to adapt their policies and pricing to a level where they could underwrite the business profitably. Ultimately, the creativity and competitive discipline of the market overcame its initial period of contraction and volatility to provide viable insurance solutions for enormous risks that were previously considered uninsurable.

The business of insurance is about measuring risks and selling promises to cover them at a reasonable profit. Insurance experts who perform these tasks are exceptionally talented. Over time, they have demonstrated a remarkable ability to adapt to unforeseen circumstances, while making available the insurance products that are essential to the growth and productivity of American business. As expected in a free competitive market, individual companies may stumble, falter, and even fail when substantial adversity strikes, but the United States insurance industry as a whole has a long and proud record of finding ways to overcome new obstacles while advancing its business goals and serving the interests of the insurance-buying public.

Thus, the NAIC believes Congress should begin its consideration of federal assistance to the insurance industry by recognizing the strength and adaptability of the private insurance markets. Federal actions that unduly disrupt or interfere with private market forces are likely to end up causing more harm than good for American consumers and federal taxpayers.

Appropriate Federal Government Action Can Help the Private Market Recover

State regulators know from their own experiences that government action can help the insurance market recover when it becomes overwhelmed by changing risk factors or catastrophic losses. When the psychology of the market results in industry reactions that harm the public, government has unique powers to alter the insurance marketplace for the benefit of consumers. We have found that successful government assistance involves tailoring actions to fix specific problems and keeping the program as narrow as possible.

Hurricane Andrew provides a useful example of limited government intervention that works. Following the tremendous losses from this hurricane in 1992, commercial reinsurers restricted their coverage for windstorms and raised prices. This caused a corresponding reaction from primary insurers, who moved to raise prices, cancel coverage for coastal properties, and increase deductible amounts for consumers having significant hurricane exposure. Within a couple of years, normalcy returned to the reinsurance market, and then to the primary market. The Florida Insurance Department assisted with the recovery of the industry by introducing a moratorium on policy cancellations and beginning the discussion of the need for a state catastrophe pool. The Florida legislature later adopted a Hurricane Catastrophe Insurance Pool that provides a state-based backstop for catastrophic windstorms in Florida. These collective actions have resulted in a robust and competitive market for homeowners insurance in the State of Florida.

In the present situation, we believe the federal government can add certainty to the market for terrorism insurance using its unique powers. For example, Congress can establish a uniform national definition of “terrorism” so that everyone is very clear what will trigger insurance coverage for acts of terrorism. Providing a temporary financial back-stop for terrorism insurance coverage is another useful step, as long as it does not allow what some have called “cherry picking” by insurers seeking to have the government cover just the most risky policies.

State insurance regulators believe the current situation affecting the availability of insurance for acts of terrorism is similar in nature to other catastrophic events. Due to the magnitude and unpredictable nature of terrorism as it is currently perceived by insurers, a temporary level of federal assistance to spread risk appropriately should provide time for the marketplace to adjust its thinking about how insurance coverage for terrorist acts should be handled. If the federal government and business customers make quick progress in lessening exposure from acts of terrorism, the insurance industry may start providing the coverage American businesses and families demand. Enacting a temporary federal solution will provide the necessary time to craft a more thoughtful long-term solution.

Important Market Factors for Congress to Keep in Mind

As Congress considers what type of federal assistance may be appropriate to steady the commercial market while it adjusts to new demands, the NAIC recommends that you keep in mind three very important factors. These factors will greatly affect the costs of any federal program, as well as its lasting impact on America’s consumers and private insurance markets.

First, risk management precautions that reduce the likelihood of losses from terrorist attacks will have a large impact on the willingness of private insurers to offer terrorism insurance coverage to customers. Risk management—meaning the implementation of safety and security measures to prevent harm—is a standard part of insuring commercial and government facilities that are most susceptible to terrorist attacks. Large firms have professional risk management departments whose mission is to reduce a company’s exposure to potential accidents and intentional harm, thereby improving the company’s chances to get insurance at the lowest rates possible.

Following the September 11th attacks, government and commercial facilities across America have added security measures to prevent acts of terrorism and limit potential damages. As commercial risk managers review these new precautions, it seems likely they will become more inclined to offer terrorism insurance because the possibility and extent of potential insured losses occurring will be greatly reduced. At that point, we expect market forces will start working to fill the gap by making terrorism insurance available through private industry.

The NAIC recommends that Congress build-in strong incentives for insurers or companies receiving federal assistance to implement and maintain effective risk management measures to prevent acts of terrorism from occurring. In that way, the federal government will be building upon standard risk-reducing steps that are well-accepted in the private marketplace for insurance products.

Second, the private market instills policyholder discipline to avoid insurance claims through the concept of co-insurance. Co-insurance means that policyholders are liable to pay part of any losses covered by insurance before expecting a recovery from an insurer. Obviously, the higher the dollar amount covered by the policyholder himself, the greater will be his incentive to take steps to avoid losses. This concept to commonly understood by everyone owning a car or a home who agrees to bear the cost of a “deductible” before receiving payment from an insurance company.

Co-insurance should be considered by Congress as an important market discipline tool that works equally well with government programs.

Third, the scope and duration of any federal assistance program will itself become a factor in the private insurance market. Even though Congress is considering special government assistance intended to operate as a supplement to normal business channels, the very fact that government will pay certain costs of a commercial business becomes a factor to be taken into account when private market decisions on terrorism insurance are made.

The NAIC urges you to keep in mind that federal government policy regarding terrorism insurance assistance will not occur in a vacuum. It will become a private market consideration affecting prices and availability of insurance, and it may impact insurance products having nothing to do with terrorism. The extent of the federal influence on private market insurance products can be expected to be directly commensurate with the size, details, and length of the federal assistance program.

State Actions Are Not Driving the Market Demand for Terrorism Insurance

The NAIC and its members have recently been asked to explain how requirements of state law impact the market demand for terrorism insurance. Many people in Congress apparently think that states require private businesses to carry insurance against terrorism, and that failure of the private insurance market to offer terrorism coverage will result in violating state laws and regulations. We believe there is a misunderstanding of what state laws require and what state insurance regulators do.

Let me say clearly that states do not drive the private market for terrorism insurance. To our knowledge, no state currently requires that business entities maintain insurance against acts of terrorism. In fact, the NAIC recently performed an electronic search of state laws and regulation for references to "terrorism". We found nothing.

Furthermore, it is important to understand that state insurance regulators do not normally get involved in the details of property/casualty insurance policies for large business operations. These are considered to be the product of free market negotiations among sophisticated insurance underwriters, brokers, and professional corporate risk managers who rely upon the traditional powers of buyers and sellers to bargain for the best deal they can get. The state regulatory interest in such large transactions is mainly that they not impair the overall financial health of an insurer, since monitoring insurer solvency is a major responsibility of regulators.

Banks and investors typically use their private market influence to require that large business and government entities maintain adequate property/casualty insurance coverage against foreseeable harm. As a result of September 11th, foreseeable harm may now start to include possible terrorist acts in addition to normal hazards. However, terrorism coverage would usually be just one part of a comprehensive insurance package that insurers want to sell. Their desire to avoid terrorist risk exposures may be offset by their need to include it in order to sell a package of insurance coverage judged to be profitable overall.

State Actions Having a Limited and Indirect Impact on Terrorism Insurance

What, then, is the impact of state laws on terrorism insurance? Primarily, it falls into three areas—workers' compensation requirements, policy form regulations, and rate regulations. We believe these areas have a limited and indirect effect upon the price and availability of terrorism coverage in commercial property/casualty policies for large business projects that significantly affect the American economy.

It is important to recognize that states do not initiate market requirements in these areas, but only react to market forces that threaten to deny consumers fair insurance coverage. In normal practice, for example, an insurer would ask a state regulator for permission to exclude a specific type of coverage, such as terrorism, when the insurer issues a policy to customers. The regulator may have general authority under state law to deny the insurer's request for the coverage exclusion as a matter of public policy, and thus force the insurer to include terrorism coverage when it sells an insurance policy. However, the insurer makes the ultimate decision as to whether it will offer an insurance policy at all, and can refuse to offer insurance policies in the state if terrorism coverage is not excluded. If enough insurers threaten to withdraw from a state's insurance market, state regulators will be under tremendous pressure to grant an exclusion for terrorism in order to keep insurers in the market providing other types of insurance.

Workers' Compensation Requirements

State workers' compensation laws were developed early in the 20th Century. In the late 1800's and early 1900's, the number of occupational injuries and illnesses occurring in the American workplace was hindering the Industrial Revolution. Businesses were asking how they could assure that working men and women who are injured on the job get the care they need, while protecting industry and commerce from the financially crippling and demoralizing prospect of employees suing their bosses for every work-related injury. The question was answered with the state workers' compensation system, which covers employees' medical expenses and lost wages for work-related injuries and disease, regardless of who was at fault. In return, employees are limited to the benefits provided by the workers' compensation system as their exclusive remedy.

State workers' compensation laws require a set of benefits that are guaranteed by employers to their employees who are injured on the job. Insurers play a key role in the delivery of the benefits promised by employers. Typically, insurers assume by contract the obligation to provide the employer's share of medical benefits, rehabilitation benefits, and survivor's benefits in exchange for premiums the employer pays the insurer. Since state law obligates the employer—and therefore the insurer that has assumed the employer's obligations—to provide the benefits specified in a state's Workers' Compensation Act, the insurer cannot introduce either an exclusion for war or an exclusion for terrorist acts.

As a no-fault safety net for workers' injuries on the job, state workers' compensation laws do not permit coverage exclusions as a matter of public policy. Workers' compensation insurance is one part of the commercial coverage maintained by significant employers.

State Policy Form Regulations

Many states have statutory authority over insurance contract language through general policy form regulations. These requirements typically prohibit contract language that is misleading, illusory, inconsistent, ambiguous, deceptive, or contrary to public policy. Since no currently enacted state laws specifically prohibit an insurer's request to exclude coverage for terrorist acts, states would have to rely upon the general provisions above if they seek to deny an insurer's request to exclude terrorism coverage. Under state law, an adverse regulatory decision can be challenged by an insurer through the state insurance department's administrative process, with the right of appeal to state courts.

State insurance regulators are also charged with solvency oversight of insurers. Thus, an action to deny an exclusion of terrorist activities under general policy form provisions could cause financial difficulties for insurance companies. However, it is ultimately the insurer's choice whether to provide coverage for a specific business event or peril. Primary insurers may be hesitant to exclude coverage for terrorist acts because they know their business and individual customers will want assurances that the coverage is provided. Reinsurers do not directly deal with businesses and families, and therefore do not face the same pressures to provide terrorism coverage.

State Rate Regulations

State rate regulations are primarily focused on protecting small businesses and individual policyholders. For commercial lines insurance products, only 13 states still require that the insurance department exercise prior approval requirement for most rate changes. The remaining 38 jurisdictions have some form of competitive rating mechanism that allows insurers to file and use rates, or use them even before they are filed with insurance regulators. Moreover, in recent years insurers have been successful in convincing state legislatures to create rate regulation exemptions for large commercial policyholders. The NAIC does not believe that state rate regulations are preventing insurers from charging adequate rates for terrorism insurance.

Conclusion

The NAIC and state regulators believe the insurance industry remains strong, and that it retains tremendous strength to recover from the September 11th attacks and adjust its business practices to new conditions in the marketplace. State insurance regulators are working together to help assure that any glitches which occur do not disrupt the process of getting people's lives back in order and America's businesses back to work. The NAIC and its members plan to work closely with Congress and fellow regulators, as set forth in the Gramm-Leach-Bliley Act, so that the needs of individual Americans and our Nation's economy are met in a timely way.

Guiding Principles for Federal Legislation Related to Property and Casualty Insurance Coverage for Losses Caused by Terrorism

The insurance industry has repeatedly encountered new, unexpected, and severe risks in the past and has always, given reasonable time and experience, been able to develop creative ways to price its products. However, certain events may exceed the capacity and willingness of the property and casualty insurance industry to provide future coverage for terrorism exposures. State insurance regulators recognize that federal legislation is urgently needed to provide a federal backstop to buttress the ability of the property and casualty insurance industry to protect Americans from financial losses associated with terrorism, while at the same time safeguarding insurer solvency so that insurance companies can continue to meet all of their other claims obligations. Outlined below are the governing principles and essential elements of any federal disaster insurance legislation that state insurance regulators support. The National Association of Insurance Commissioners (NAIC) urges Congress to take immediate action to enact legislation consistent with these principles.

For purposes of this document, the use of the word "terrorism" includes the war risk for workers' compensation that insurers are required to provide coverage for as a result of statutory provisions contained in state workers' compensation laws.

A. The Role of a Federal Government Program

1. Federal legislation in this area should "sunset" at a date certain of limited duration after enactment in order to allow a reevaluation of the need for and design of the program.
2. To take advantage of the substantial experience of state-based insurance regulation, the expertise of the NAIC should be made available to any federal program in this area and consideration should be given to including representatives of the NAIC as members of the governing body of such a program.

B. The Content of a Federal Program

3. Federal legislation should supplement but not replace other private and public insurance mechanisms where those mechanisms can provide coverage more efficiently.
4. Federal legislation should include clear and non-ambiguous definitions of terrorism to be applied to all policies nationwide.
5. Rates should consider all reasonable factors that can be feasibly measured and supported by theoretical and empirical analysis, including relative risk.
6. Federal legislation should encourage loss reduction and hazard mitigation efforts.
7. State residual market mechanisms and other pooling mechanisms providing coverage should be allowed to participate in any program established by federal legislation but in such a way as to not create incentives for business to be placed in those residual markets.
8. Federal legislation should recognize that terrorism exposures subject insurers to potential "adverse selection," *i.e.*, entities with lower risk are less likely to voluntarily purchase coverage, while those with greater risk are more likely to purchase coverage. If possible, the federal program should encourage the inclusion of both low-risk and high-risk entities to promote greater risk spreading in a way that does not subject risk-bearing entities, including the federal government, to adverse selection.
9. Federal legislation should address coverage and cost for all risks exposed to terrorism, regardless of geographic, demographic or other classification, such as "more-at-risk" or "less-at-risk."
10. There should be a safety net protection, within reasonable limits, for any private program created by federal legislation in the event of the insolvency of the program or its participants.
11. Tax law changes should be encouraged to avoid penalties on and encourage the accumulation of reserves for the portion of terrorism losses insurable in the private marketplace.
12. Federal legislation should not unnecessarily preempt state authority.

C. Participation in the Program

13. Federal legislation should encourage individuals and businesses to maintain private coverage for terrorism exposure.
14. Federal legislation should promote or encourage awareness that coverage is available for any property and/or casualty risk that meets reasonable standards of insurability.
15. Federal legislation should encourage or mandate that eligible entities participate in the program or run the risk of losing access to federal disaster assistance.

D. Administration of the Program

16. There should be an appropriate balance of the different private and public interests in the governance of regulatory oversight over the program.
17. Federal legislation should recognize the expertise of the states in insurance regulation with respect to such areas as licensing insurers, solvency surveillance, oversight of rates and forms in most jurisdictions, licensing producers, assisting policyholders and consumers during the claim settlement process and performing market conduct examinations.

18. To more efficiently achieve the objectives of any federal terrorism program, there should be coordination of state and federal regulatory responsibilities.

19. Jurisdiction over insurer claim settlement practices should remain with the states.

Senator NELSON. (presiding) Mr. Keating, later on, when we get to questions, I want you to talk about what appropriate role you think the federal government would play, and Ms. Koken, if you will discuss later on the question of the concern of the State Insurance Commissioners of basically federalizing insurance regulations.

Mr. HAWKINS.

STATEMENT OF MR. PHILLIP L. HAWKINS, CHIEF OPERATING OFFICER, CARR AMERICA REALTY CORPORATION

Mr. HAWKINS. Good afternoon. Thank you for the opportunity to be here today. I am Phil Hawkins, Chief Operating Officer of CarrAmerica Realty Corporation, a New York Stock Exchange company that owns, develops, and operates office properties in 14 markets throughout the United States.

I am intimately familiar with the impact of terrorist threats from some private properties, since CarrAmerica is one of the largest commercial landlords in downtown Washington, D.C. and owns and operates office buildings across the street from the Old Executive Office Building.

I am here today as a member of the National Association of Real Estate Investment Trusts, and on behalf of a number of real estate organizations and trade groups that are separately submitting written testimony.

The tragic events of September 11 have triggered a withdrawal of virtually all new property and casualty insurance coverage relating to terrorism. While this will become more readily apparent throughout the economy on January 1, when approximately 70 percent of the policies on commercial properties are scheduled for renewal, it is already causing significant problems in pending real estate transactions.

As the COO of CarrAmerica, I know from my more than 20 years of experience that it is not possible to buy, sell, or finance property unless it is adequately covered by insurance. A significant percentage of privately owned properties which are open to the public, including shopping centers, office buildings, and hotels, will need to renew their insurance coverage on January 1.

Many of these owners have been advised that their policies may not be renewed, or that the new policies will exclude exposures currently insured, including terrorism. These owners have also been advised that while they will have to absorb significant increases in their premiums, they will also bear expanded uninsured exposures due to new policy exclusions. Without adequate insurance, it will be difficult, if not impossible to develop, operate, or acquire properties, refinance loans, and to sell commercial-backed securities.

The disappearance of coverage for terrorist acts on real estate and its effects on other businesses could several disrupt the economy. It will not only affect real estate owners and lenders, but also, most importantly, the tenants who lease facilities, their employees and customers, as well as anyone who rents an apartment. I am very concerned about the short and long-term future of the real estate industry unless the federal government creates some type of mechanism to help provide this coverage.

Up to September 11, property and general liability policies typically covered losses, including business interruption costs stemming from terrorism and similar acts. However, as confirmed by recent insurance industry CEO's testimony, future policies will exclude coverage for terrorism and sabotage, in addition to the current exclusion for acts of war.

Additionally, they stated that reinsurance for terrorism and sabotage is currently unavailable in the marketplace. Without reinsurance, there will likely be no primary insurance covering losses caused by terrorism. As a result, the real estate and construction industries, which account for over a quarter of the Nation's gross domestic product, could face severe economic dislocation in the coming months if the federal government does not immediately address insurance-related issues tied to terrorism.

The federal government needs to help ensure that commercial property owners and other businesses can continue to obtain insurance coverage to losses related to terrorism in the future. It will become an increasingly larger problem if it is not resolved prior to the expiration of the many policies that terminate on January 1. Necessary characteristics of a workable plan include the following.

First, duration. Because real property is a long-lived, fixed asset, it is generally financed for a long term, typically 10 to 30 years. Thus, if the program created is of insufficient length, it may not provide sufficient stability in the long term. Any program created must be of sufficient duration to provide reasonable certainty for these long-term owners, lenders, and investors. If congress decides to adopt a program of just 2 to 3 years, it is important to provide the President with the flexibility to extend the program if he makes a finding that the private markets cannot offer terrorism coverage at that point.

Second, definition of terrorism. The line between terrorism and acts of war has been blurred significantly since September 11. President Bush and the news media have been focused on our current war against terrorism. The real estate industry is concerned that any future incidents in this ongoing conflict may be considered an act of war by the insurance industry and therefore excluded from coverage. Accordingly, any program created must cover an expansive notion of terrorism so that future events along the lines of September 11 and other similar acts are covered and are not excluded from coverage in the future.

Third, deductible limits of coverage. The real estate industry is concerned that a dramatic and insupportable increase in deductibles to property owners could be tantamount to no insurance coverage at all. For example, if a real estate owner plans to acquire a $10 million property with $3 million of equity and $7 million of debt, a total loss under an insurance policy with a deductible of $3 million or more could effectively wipe out that real estate owner's equity and would likely not result in an investment in the property. The same result would likely arise if the insurer kept the policy limit at $7 million. That would not protect the owner's equity.

Fourth, disclosure of premium cost. With property and casualty insurance rates already predicted to sky rocket prior to the attack on America, insurers should be required to disclose the cost of coverage before any misunderstanding as to the program's impact on overall insurance rates. Otherwise, it will be impossible to discern the actual increase in the policy as a result of the difficulty in writing terrorism coverage and the increase as a result of other market conditions. Our congress must not fail to act. Our industry welcomes the opportunity to work with the administration and congress to achieve a workable solution to this immediate problem this year, and our company wants to get back to its core mission of creating a better place to live, learn, work, travel, and play.

Thank you.

[The statement of Mr. Hawkins follows:]

PREPARED STATEMENT OF PHILIP L. HAWKINS, CHIEF OPERATING OFFICER, CARRAMERICA REALTY CORPORATION

Thank you for the opportunity to be here today. My name is Phil Hawkins, and I am the Chief Operating Officer of CarrAmerica Realty Corporation, a New York Stock Exchange company that owns, develops and operates office properties in 14 markets throughout the United States. I am intimately familiar with the impact of terrorist threats on private property since CarrAmerica is one of the largest commercial landlords in downtown Washington, D.C. and owns and operates office buildings across the street from the Old Executive Office Building. I am here today as a member of the National Association of Real Estate Investment Trusts and on behalf of a number of real estate organizations and trade groups that are separately submitting written testimony.

The tragic events of September 11th have triggered a withdrawal of virtually all new property and casualty insurance coverage relating to terrorism. While this will become more readily apparent throughout the economy on January 1st, when approximately 70 percent of the policies on commercial properties are scheduled for renewal, it is already causing significant problems in pending real estate transactions.

As the COO of CarrAmerica, I know from my more than 20 years of experience that it is not possible to buy, sell or finance a property unless it is adequately covered by insurance. A significant percentage of privately owned properties which are open to the public, including shopping centers, offices and hotels will need to renew their insurance coverage on January 1st. Many of these owners have been advised that their policies may not be renewed or that their new policies will exclude exposures currently insured including terrorism. These owners have also been advised that while they will have to absorb significant increases in their premiums, they will also bear expanded uninsured exposures due to new policy exclusions.

Without adequate insurance, it will be difficult, if not impossible, to develop, operate or acquire properties, refinance loans, and to sell commercial-backed securities. Disappearance of coverage for terrorist acts on real estate and its effect on other businesses could severely disrupt the economy. It will not only affect real estate owners and lenders but also their tenants who lease facilities, their employees and customers as well as anyone who rents an apartment. I am very concerned about the short and long-term future of the real estate industry unless the Federal government creates some type of mechanism to help provide this coverage.

Before September 11, property and general liability policies typically covered losses including business interruption costs stemming from terrorism and similar acts. However, as confirmed by recent insurance industry CEOs' testimony, future policies will exclude coverage for terrorism and sabotage in addition to their current exclusion for acts of war. Additionally, they stated that reinsurance for terrorism and sabotage is currently unavailable in the marketplace. Without reinsurance, there will likely be no primary insurance covering losses caused by terrorism. As a result, the real estate and construction industries, which account for over a quarter of the nation's gross domestic product, could face severe economic dislocation in the coming months if the federal government does not immediately address insurance-related issues tied to terrorism.

The Federal government needs to help ensure that commercial property owners and other businesses can continue to obtain insurance coverage for losses related to terrorism in the future. It will become an increasingly larger problem if it is not resolved prior to the expiration of the many policies that terminate on January 1. Necessary characteristics of a workable plan include the following:

—**Duration:** Because real property is a long-lived fixed asset, it is generally financed over a long-term—typically 10–30 years. Thus, if the program created is of insufficient length, it may not provide sufficient stability in the long-term. Any program created must be of sufficient duration to provide reasonable certainty for these long-term owners, lenders and investors. If Congress decides to adopt a program of just 2 to 3 years, it is important to provide the President with the flexibility to extend the program if he makes a finding that the private markets cannot offer terrorism coverage at that point.

—**Definition of Terrorism:** The line between "terrorism" and "acts of war" has been blurred significantly since the September 11 attacks on the World Trade Center and the Pentagon. President Bush and news media have been focused on our current "war against terrorism." The real estate industry is concerned that any future incidents in this ongoing conflict may be considered an "act of war" by the insurance industry and therefore be excluded from coverage. Accordingly, any program created must cover an expansive notion of terrorism so that future events along the lines of September 11 and other similar acts are covered—and are not excluded from coverage in the future.

—**Deductible/Limits of Coverage:** The real estate industry is concerned that a dramatic and unsupportable increase in deductibles to property owners could be tantamount to no insurance coverage at all. For example, if a real estate owner plans to acquire a $10 million property with $3 million of equity and $7 million of debt, a total loss under an insurance policy with a deductible of $3 million or more could effectively wipe out the real estate owner's equity and would likely not result in an investment in the property. The same result would likely arise if the insurer capped the policy limit at $7 million that would not protect the owner's equity. Accordingly, any program created must carefully consider apportionment of loss exposure among property owners, lenders, insurers and the Federal government.

—**Disclosure of Premium Cost:** With property and casualty insurance rates already predicted to skyrocket prior to the attack on America, insurers should be required to separately disclose the cost of terrorism coverage to avoid any misunderstanding as to the program's impact on overall insurance rates. Otherwise, it will be impossible to discern the actual increase in the policy as a result of the difficulty in writing terrorism coverage and the increase as result of other market conditions.

Our Congress must not fail to act. Our industry welcomes the opportunity to work with the Administration and Congress to achieve a workable solution to this immediate problem this year and our company wants to get back to its core mission of "creating better places to live, learn, work, travel and play".

Senator NELSON. Mr. Hawkins, you need available and affordable insurance is basically your testimony.

Mr. HAWKINS. Yes.

Senator NELSON. You do not care how that is among the various proposals that have been proffered here?

Mr. HAWKINS. I am not a student of the various proposals, quite honestly. We just need a mechanism to ensure that affordable insurance is available, because that has a direct impact not only on us as owners but, frankly, on our tenants. The cost of the insurance is really passed through to them directly by contract, so yes.

Senator NELSON. Mr. Moss.

Mr. MOSS. Thank you, Mr. Chairman.

Senator NELSON. Excuse me. Senator Fitzgerald.

Senator FITZGERALD. I would like to ask a quick question of Mr. Hawkins before we go on to the next witness. At your business, CarrAmerica Realty Corporation, in many of your commercial office building leases do you have a clause permitting you to pass through increases in the cost of real estate taxes to your tenants?

Mr. HAWKINS. Yes.

Senator FITZGERALD. Do you also have a clause providing that you may pass through the cost of an increase in property and casualty insurance?

Mr. HAWKINS. Yes, sir.

Senator FITZGERALD. So you can pass the cost of your increased premiums through to your tenants?

Mr. HAWKINS. Yes.

Senator FITZGERALD. Okay. Are there any buildings that you own where you cannot pass that cost through to your tenants?

Mr. HAWKINS. Well, there are two issues. One is, any cost increase in the short run will definitely impact the existing tenants in those businesses. 80 percent of our tenants are small businesses, 40 employees or less, so that cost is passed to them immediately and directly.

Over time, though, as those tenants have choices, unless all insurance goes up identically they will certainly move from one part of the country to another, one city to another, whatever.

Senator FITZGERALD. They might be working out of their homes, too.

Mr. HAWKINS. Cost of rent will go up.

Senator FITZGERALD. So basically, all of those increased premiums that you would incur would be passed along to your tenants.

Mr. HAWKINS. By contract, yes.

Senator FITZGERALD. I just want to be clear on that. Senator Nelson: Mr. Moss.

STATEMENT OF MR. DAVID MOSS, ASSOCIATE PROFESSOR, HARVARD BUSINESS SCHOOL

Mr. MOSS. Thank you, Mr. Chairman. In his letter, Senator Hollings asked me to consider, "the role the federal government should play, if any, in identifying terrorism related risks". As it happens, I have just finished writing a book exploring the government's role as a risk manager, and tracing the history of that role here in the United States. So I want to start by saying just a little bit about what the historical record suggests.

One thing my research makes clear is that there is nothing at all unusual about the government getting involved in allocating or absorbing private-sector risk. Policymakers at the state and federal levels have been managing all sorts of risks since the very earliest days of the Republic, in policies ranging from limited liability law to federal deposit insurance to Social Security. I would be glad to explain it in greater detail, if you are interested. But suffice it to say here that the current notion of involving the federal government in the management of terror-related risks would in no way constitute a radical departure from the path of American policymaking.

What the historical record also makes clear, however, is that some risk-management policies have worked considerably better than others. The biggest problems, in my view, have involved open-ended government guarantees, which actually end up encouraging risky behavior. I am afraid our experience with federal disaster policy is a case in point.

The bottom line is that government can play an extremely constructive role in managing risk when the private market falters. And it has done this in many different circumstances. But we have to be very careful in the way we structure these policies so as not to distort incentives and reduce safety. That in a nutshell is what the historical record tells us.

Now, the problem at hand is that terror-related losses, as you well know, could become uninsurable in the aftermath of September 11, with insurers and reinsurers threatening to withdraw from the private market altogether. This in itself is obviously a serious problem. But in addition, as others have mentioned and as the Secretary has mentioned, the collateral economic damage from a breakdown in the insurance market could be immense.

So how do we address this? Ideally, I think we should work to fashion a public policy that ensures a working market for terror risk, but with as little subsidy as possible. I want to emphasize that again, because I think it may have been lost. We want to ensure a working market for terror risk, but we want to do it with as little subsidy as possible. At least, that is what I believe. And this means steering clear of open-ended federal guarantees like the ones implicit in federal disaster policy and the ones, unfortunately, that the Banking Committee and the White House seem to favor in this case.

Not only are these sorts of guarantees expensive, they are potentially dangerous as well. They are also remarkably difficult, if not impossible, to eliminate once they are in place.

Instead of open-ended guarantees, therefore, I believe we should try to follow a more explicit model of reinsurance for terror-related risks, where the government would demand risk-based premiums in return for the coverage it provides. I think we can do that.

I have outlined a specific policy proposal in my written testimony. But before I conclude, I want to highlight three primary advantages of this reinsurance approach. First, I am confident that the creation of a well-structured federal reinsurance program would solve the central problem we face today by ensuring that private coverage against terror risk would continue to be written in the coming months and years. I think we can solve that problem.

Second, this reinsurance approach (where premiums were demanded in return for the risk that was covered) would exploit the inherent strengths of the private market. It would place private insurers on the front lines, which is where they belong, tapping their enormous capabilities in risk assessment, risk monitoring, and policy administration. But perhaps most important of all, unlike any of the other major proposals under consideration, it would ensure that nearly all of the risk being covered was appropriately priced in the private market, minimizing any distortion of market incentives. I believe this is absolutely critical. It is not only a question of cost and fiscal responsibility. It is absolutely critical because the proper incentives are what make us safe. Distorted incentives invite unsafe construction, they invite second-rate security operations, and they invite a whole host of other problems that would compromise our safety. Getting the prices right, the price of insurance right, means safety, pure and simple.

Finally, under the public reinsurance plan I am proposing, the federal government's role would automatically recede if private insurers and reinsurers chose to assume more of the risk on their own. We would not even need a sunset provision. So it would complement, not replace the private market. I would be glad to explain that, further, if necessary.

Obviously, no plan is perfect. But I favor a program of reinsurance for terror-related risks because, in my view, it would combine the best of both public and private. It would draw on the government's unique and rather extraordinary strengths as a risk manager, but it would do so without short-circuiting either the essential capabilities or, and I think this is most important, the relentless discipline of the private market.

I think it would come as close as is possible at the present time to making this broken market whole and therefore restoring a precious source of security in our economic life.

Thank you.

[The statement of Mr. Moss follows:]

PREPARED STATEMENT OF DAVID A. MOSS, ASSOCIATE PROFESSOR, HARVARD BUSINESS SCHOOL

Thank you Senator Hollings and Senator McCain for the opportunity to address the committee today.

I. The Government's Role as a Risk Manager

In his letter of invitation, Senator Hollings asked me to consider "the role the Federal government should play, if any, in indemnifying terrorism related risks. . . ."

Since I have just finished writing a book that traces the history of government efforts to manage risk, let me start by saying just a little bit about what the historical record suggests.[1]

Contrary to popular wisdom, government involvement with private-sector risks is nothing new. American lawmakers have been managing all sorts of risks since the earliest days of the Republic. Many of these government policies are so firmly entrenched that we take them for granted. Limited liability, for example, was first enacted at the state level beginning in the early nineteenth century and has since emerged as one of the hallmarks of modern corporation law. Yet limited liability is really nothing more than a simple risk management device, shifting part of the risk of corporate default from shareholders to creditors. Federal deposit insurance is another major risk management policy. Inaugurated during the Great Depression, this federal program safeguards individual depositors by spreading the risk of bank failure across all depositors and potentially across all taxpayers as well.

Other notable risk-management policies include federal bankruptcy law, workers' compensation, unemployment insurance, old-age insurance, product liability law, state insurance guaranty funds, federal foreign-investment insurance, and federal disaster relief. Still other examples involve federal caps on liability, such as the cap on nuclear power liability enacted in 1957 (Price-Anderson) and the cap on credit card liability established in 1970. One thing that these diverse policies have in common is that they all reallocate private-sector risks.

In a great many cases, such risk-management policies were introduced because lawmakers concluded that private markets for risk weren't functioning adequately on their own. As early as 1818, for example, Representative Ezekiel Whitman of Massachusetts focused on the problem of uninsurability as a reason for enacting a special bankruptcy law for merchants. "Every effort of the merchant is surrounded with danger . . ." he noted. "Gentlemen have said that the merchant may insure. . . . He may insure against sea risks and capture. But are these all the risks to which the merchant is liable? Indeed they are not. The risks which overwhelm him are more frequently and almost always, those against which he can have no

[1] David A. Moss, *When All Else Fails: Government as the Ultimate Risk Manager* (Cambridge: Harvard University Press, forthcoming 2002).

[private] insurance."[2] Such logic—emphasizing the government's role as a risk manager in a world of imperfect markets for risk—has helped to produce some of our most enduring and vital public policies, from bankruptcy law to Social Security.

Based on this history, I think it is fair to say that the prospect of involving the federal government in the management of terror-related risks would in no way constitute a radical departure from the path of American policymaking.

What the historical record also makes clear, however, is that some risk-management policies have worked considerably better than others. Policies like limited liability law, federal deposit insurance, and even the cap on credit card liability have worked remarkably well. Some others have worked less well. Federal disaster policy, for instance, has probably proved unnecessarily costly by encouraging construction in hazard-prone areas.

There are many factors that serve to distinguish relatively successful risk-management policies from less successful ones. But perhaps the most important factor is the degree to which risk taking can be effectively monitored within the confines of the policy. Whenever risk is shifted from one party to another—whether through an insurance contract, some other financial transaction, or a government program—the party that sees its risk reduced may have an incentive to engage in additional risk taking. Economists call this moral hazard. Private insurers have long recognized that controlling moral hazard requires that they carefully monitor their clients. In writing commercial fire insurance, for example, they may require the regular inspection of sprinklers and other safety devices. The same basic principle applies in the case of government risk management as well. Unless some sort of monitoring—either by public or private actors—is built into a risk management policy, moral hazard is liable to spin out of control.

Fortunately, this sort of monitoring is built into a large number of our risk management policies. In some cases, incentives are created for private actors to do the monitoring. Limited liability for corporate shareholders works well because, in most cases, corporate risk taking is effectively monitored by private creditors, such as bankers and bondholders. In other cases, the government itself does the monitoring. Federal deposit insurance provides a good example, since government regulators help to limit potential moral hazard by actively monitoring bank risk. Significantly, one of the most striking failures of federal banking policy came in the 1980s, when federal oversight of the S&L's was relaxed at the same time that federal insurance coverage was actually increased. For the most part, however, federal monitoring of bank risk has proved reasonably effective over the years.

Unfortunately, effective risk monitoring has never been a major part of federal disaster policy, leaving it exceptionally vulnerable to moral hazard. To be sure, the emergency appropriations that Congress has consistently approved in the aftermath of major disasters have relieved—and even prevented—a great deal of suffering and distress; and they have helped facilitate and accelerate recovery in devastated areas. But there has been precious little success in fashioning a disaster policy in this country that would help to control reckless building and other risky behavior that ultimately compound disaster losses. Indeed, the disaster relief itself has probably increased this sort of behavior.

In the wake of the great Mississippi flood of 1993, which triggered over $6 billion in federal relief, Representative Fred Grandy of Iowa observed, "We're basically telling people, 'We want you to buy insurance, but if you don't, we'll bail you out anyway.'" Similarly, Representative Patricia Schroeder of Colorado noted that as "we watch this tremendously awful flood scene unravel in the Midwest . . . we are going to have make some very difficult choices. One of the main choices will be: Do we help those who took responsibility, got flood insurance, put up levees, tried to do everything they could; or do we help those who did not do that, who risked it all and figured if all fails, the Federal Government will bail them out."[3] Sadly, federal disaster policy has never adequately addressed this challenge.

It is said that the path into the harbor is marked by sunken ships. My hope is that Congress and the President will successfully navigate around the defects of federal disaster policy in crafting a program that facilitates the efficient management of terror-related risks in the aftermath of September 11th. If the federal government

---

[2] Quoted in Moss, *When All Else Fails*, chap. 5. Although a federal bankruptcy law was not passed in 1818, the logic that Representative Whitman articulated helped to form the foundation of modern bankruptcy law. "A right to a fresh start," writes bankruptcy scholar Douglas Baird, ". . . is a kind of insurance. All debtors pay a higher rate of interest at the outset and, in return, the creditor bears part of the loss that arises when a particular debtor falls on hard times" [Douglas G. Baird, *The Elements of Bankruptcy* (Westbury, NY: Foundation Press, 1993), p. 33].

[3] Quoted in Moss, *When All Else Fails*, chap. 9.

is going to assume responsibility for bearing some part of the risk that is currently borne by private insurers, it is essential that the resulting public policy provides for the effective monitoring of risky behavior—either through outright regulation or, better yet, well structured incentives.

The history of risk management policy demonstrates unmistakably that government can serve an enormously constructive role as a risk manager. But the historical record also provides a warning about the problems that can ensue from open-ended risk-absorption policies that impose little in the way of discipline and ultimately look more like simple subsidies than anything else. This, it seems to me, is the proper context in which to take up the problem at hand.

II. Insurance After September 11th: Defining the Problem

One of the many ramifications of the horror of September 11th is that the market for insurance against terror-related risks has been severely disrupted. Some say it is on the verge of collapse. A report put out by Tillinghast-Towers Perrin estimates that insured losses stemming from the September 11th attack will be between $30 and $58 billion, making it "the largest single-event loss in history."[4]

An event of this magnitude affects the insurance market in two separate, though related, ways. First, our expectations about future losses stemming from terrorist attacks obviously increase substantially. And this implies that even if insurance and reinsurance providers were willing to continue covering terror-related risks, with no disruption in service, the cost of such coverage would rise sharply for many policyholders. There can be little doubt that the cost of insuring a skyscraper like the Sears Tower should increase substantially as a result of our new knowledge about the risks of terrorism. In some cases, insurance could prove prohibitively expensive, destroying the economic viability of certain business endeavors.

A second—and even more disturbing—consequence is that terror-related risks could be rendered uninsurable in the private marketplace. The magnitude of the September 11th catastrophe has forced insurers and reinsurers to think seriously about previously unimaginable events (or series of events), some of which could conceivably swamp their reserves. Although the combined resources of the insurance industry are obviously very large, they are nonetheless finite.

A closely related concern is that there is now enormous uncertainty about how to estimate the probabilities of future terror-related losses. According to most insurance textbooks, one of the preconditions for insurability is that expected losses can be estimated with a fair degree of confidence. "For an exposure to loss to be insurable," reads one prominent textbook, "the expected loss must be calculable. Ideally, this means that there is a determinable probability distribution for losses within a reasonable degree of accuracy. . . . When the probability distribution of losses for the exposure to be insured against cannot be accurately calculated, the risk is uninsurable."[5]

In explaining their intention to withdraw from covering terror-related risks in the absence of government backing, many insurance and reinsurance executives have cited precisely this combination of factors: the extraordinary magnitudes of potential losses involved and the near impossibility of accurately estimating loss probabilities. Said the Chubb Corporation's Chairman and CEO Dean R. O'Hare at a recent congressional hearing, "The industry has a specific amount of capital and cannot insure risks that are infinite and impossible to price."[6]

The business community thus faces two distinct problems in obtaining coverage for terror-related risks in the wake of September 11th—high cost on the one hand and uninsurability on the other. Even under the best of circumstances, such coverage would likely become far more expensive than it was before the tragedy, raising costs for many businesses and potentially forcing some under water. Under the worst of circumstances, such coverage would be unobtainable at any price, severely disrupting numerous markets but especially real estate.

Assuming that federal lawmakers wished to address either one of these problems, the former (high cost of terror insurance) would require some sort of government subsidy, whereas the latter (uninsurability) would require the government to act as a risk manager, perhaps providing terror insurance itself or facilitating its provision in the private sector. Although these two problems—high cost and uninsurability—

---

[4] Tillinghast-Towers Perrin, *Why Do We Need Federal Reinsurance for Terrorism?* (October 8, 2001).

[5] James L. Athearn, S. Travis Pritchett, and Joan T. Schmit, *Risk and Insurance*, 6th ed. (St. Paul: West Publishing Company, 1989), p. 57. On the fundamental distinction between risk (which is measurable) and uncertainty (which is not), see Frank H. Knight, *Risk, Uncertainty, and Profit* (Chicago: University of Chicago Press, 1971 [1921]), esp. p. 233.

[6] "U.S. Securities and Insurance Industries: Keeping the Promise," Hearing of the House Financial Services Committee, September 26, 2001.

are obviously linked in the current crisis, I believe it is useful to think about them separately when contemplating a potential policy response.

III. Fashioning a Policy Response

Ideally, I believe we should work to fashion a public policy that ensures a working market for terror risk with as little subsidy as possible. That is, we should try to address the sources of uninsurability, to the extent that they exist, while working hard to avoid any action that would make the private costs of terror-related risks look smaller than they really are.

To return for a moment to the example of federal disaster policy: one of the consequences of repeatedly providing ad hoc disaster coverage (relief) that is not tied to any sort of premium is that it ends up encouraging construction in unsafe areas, such as flood zones. That is because those who live in these areas often do not have to bear anything like the full actuarial costs. Federal disaster policy, in other words, helps to manage a wide range of risks, some of which might otherwise be uninsurable in the private marketplace. But it also ends up subsidizing those in the highest risk areas, since federally covered losses are funded not out of experience-rated premiums but rather out of general government revenues. Although some degree of subsidy is probably inevitable in any public policy designed to address disaster losses, our own federal disaster policy seems to carry the practice to an undesirable extreme.

In constructing a federal policy to facilitate the coverage of terror-related risks, one way to avoid these pitfalls would be to follow a more explicit model of insurance or reinsurance, where the government demands risk-based premiums in return for the coverage it provides. Although private insurers and reinsurers have expressed doubts about their ability to cover future terror-related risks, the federal government is ideally suited to underwrite precisely this sort of risk. Unlike private entities, the federal government is well positioned to absorb even massive losses because it enjoys the power to tax as well as a near-perfect credit rating. If the premiums it had collected were not sufficient to cover a particular loss, whether because of simple bad luck or misestimation of the risk, it could always draw the needed funds from general revenues and then recalibrate its insurance (or reinsurance) program after the fact. As FDR's Secretary of Labor, Frances Perkins, once said of the Social Security old-age-insurance program, "we have the credit of the Government as the real underlying reserve. That is what gives this stability."[7]

One of the biggest challenges in constructing a federal program for insuring or reinsuring terror risk would be to figure out how best to set premiums, so as to avoid excessive cross-subsidization and thus the distortion of traditional market incentives. Another challenge would be to structure the program so that the federal role would automatically shrink if private insurers and reinsurers ever demonstrated a willingness to reassume the burden.

One option, which I favor, would be to establish a new federal reinsurance program for terror-related risks. Primary insurers that met appropriate standards would be permitted to reinsure terror risk with the federal government. Under such a program, a primary insurer might be allowed to pass (at its discretion) between, say, 20 and 80 percent of its terror-related risk—along with the same percentage of the premiums it charged—to the federal government. Ideally, the primary insurer would also be able to purchase some sort of federal stop-loss protection on the portion of risk it retained.[8]

There are three main advantages of this federal reinsurance approach:

> First, by allowing insurers to cede a substantial portion of terror risk to the federal government and by setting an absolute ceiling on their terror-related losses (through stop-loss protection), a federal reinsurance program would ensure that coverage against terrorism would continue to be written in the aftermath of September 11th.
>
> Second, this approach would exploit the inherent strengths of the private market. Since primary insurers would remain responsible for writing terrorism policies, setting premiums, and retaining at least a portion of the risk, a federal reinsurance program would make effective use of their un-

[7] Quoted in Moss, *When All Else Fails*, chap. 7.

[8] Public reinsurance programs of this sort have been tried, often with considerable success, in other countries. Most notable are Britain's Pool Reinsurance Company, which covers terrorism risk, and France's Caisse Centrale de Réassurance, which covers natural catastrophe risk. On the former, see Tillinghast-Towers Perrin, "Pool Re and Terrorism Insurance in Great Britain," October 2001; and on the latter, see David A. Moss, "Courting Disaster? The Transformation of Federal Disaster Policy since 1803," in Kenneth A. Froot, ed., *The Financing of Catastrophe Risk* (Chicago: University of Chicago Press, 1999), esp. pp. 345–351.

paralleled capabilities in risk assessment, risk monitoring, and policy administration. Perhaps most important, nearly all of the covered risk—even that portion ceded to the government reinsurer—would be appropriately priced in the private marketplace, thus minimizing any distortion of vital market incentives. Developers who wished to build skyscrapers or other structures that insurers deemed unusually vulnerable to terrorist attack might be deterred from doing so by the prospect of exceptionally high insurance premiums. As a result, there would be little need for additional federal regulation to monitor risk taking and control moral hazard. Risk-based premiums, combined with monitoring by private insurers, would likely prove sufficient.[9]

Finally, under a public reinsurance plan of this sort, the federal government's role would automatically recede if private insurers and reinsurers chose to assume more of the risk. Not only would participating insurers be free to increase their retention levels as desired (up to 80 percent), but they would also be free to withdraw from the program entirely or to obtain coverage from private reinsurers if the latter ever reentered the market. Competition, in other words, would be encouraged rather than stifled.

While no plan is perfect, I favor a program of federal reinsurance for terrorism-related risks because, in my view, it would combine the best of both public and private, drawing on the government's unique strengths as a risk manager without short-circuiting either the essential capabilities or the relentless discipline of the private market. It would come as close as is possible at the present time to making a broken market whole and restoring a precious source of security in our economic life.

Senator NELSON. Thank you, Mr. Moss. Mr. Plunkett.

STATEMENT OF MR. TRAVIS PLUNKETT, LEGISLATIVE DIRECTOR, CONSUMER FEDERATION OF AMERICA

Mr. PLUNKETT. Thank you, Mr. Chairman, members of the committee. Thank you for holding this hearing on such an important topic. I am Travis Plunkett. I am the Legislative Director for the Consumer Federation of America.

I will be offering my comments today for our Director of Insurance, Bob Hunter, who is unfortunately out of the country. Bob is uniquely qualified to comment on the various reinsurance proposals you have heard, because he developed the rate structure for the Federal Riot Reinsurance Program Senator Fitzgerald mentioned as a Federal Administrator. He is also a former State Insurance Commissioner.

Let me be clear about our position. The Consumer Federation does support a federal backup of the insurance business for the peril of terrorism. We have offered several principles in our written testimony that should be used to measure whether any plan for terrorism coverage is fair to consumers and taxpayers. Measured against these principles, both versions of the administration plan as well as the industry plan have serious flaws.

First, they do not require actuarial soundness. Indeed, insurers would pay nothing for reinsurance for at least the first year of the industry program, and never under the initial administration approach. Based on news reports, it appears that the revised Treasury plan, the compromise legislation we have heard about today,

[9] By contrast, a government policy that simply capped insurer liability at some arbitrary figure (such as $10 billion) without assessing a premium for the associated government guaranty would encourage insurers to underprice terror risk, thus inviting the construction of new buildings and the pursuit of other business activities that under normal market conditions might have been deemed too dangerous (*i.e.*, too vulnerable to terrorist attack) to be economically viable. By distorting critical market incentives, in other words, such a policy could compromise our safety.

will require first dollar federal coverage. That is better, but the plan still is an unwarranted handout and a burden on taxpayers if it does not mandate the payment of premiums by the industry or any loan repayment requirements.

There is absolutely no reason not to make the taxpayer whole when property casualty insurers are still well capitalized, have a very large surplus, and the target risks that would be insured are relatively large and wealthy.

Second, none of the plans that have been offered are simple enough to be up and running on January 1 of next year, when the bulk of private reinsurance against the perils of terrorism expired. The insurer plan is worse than the administration plan, in that it proposes an end of rate regulation and would override any remnant of state or federal antitrust laws. They also want to sweep tort reform into their proposal. Another important point is neither insurer nor administration plans assure affordability or availability of coverage to reasonably secure risks.

The Consumer Federation has offered what we believe to be a better approach that is elegantly simple. Since the vast majority of insurers could withstand at least another event of the magnitude of the September 11 tragedy, God forbid, we are sure that the plan need not cover first dollar losses. CFA proposes that a retention for each insurer of 5 percent of surplus be used. This protects weaker insurers from insolvency risk and minimizes interference with insurance pricing decisions.

Terrorism, and we agree with much of what you have heard on the definition of terrorism, would then have to be carefully defined, and a federal official should determine the availability of loans by the government to insurers under this definition. If a terrorist attack occurs and an insurer suffers a claim greater than 5 percent of surplus retention, the insurer would then be eligible for federal low or no cost loans, the term of which would be negotiated up to 30 years. this would spread the cost over time, an important goal. For each insurer, the discounted value of the loan would be limited to an additional 5 percent of that insurer's surplus. This limit is needed in order to make sure that individual company balance sheets are not affected by very large losses due to terrorist activity.

Amounts of money loaned in excess of 10 percent of surplus by a company would be repaid to the U.S. Treasury through a property casualty insurance industry-wide loan repayment mechanism. This loan repayment would be collected over a number of years sufficient to minimize the rate impact to consumers, who will ultimately pay the cost of the program. Congress should set the maximum surcharge, perhaps at 2.5 percent per year, until the loan is repaid. The surcharge would be collected by the states as a piggyback on their premium tax mechanism and forwarded to the Treasury.

This plan—and this is a very important point. It leaves the regulation of insurance fully in state hands. The states should be required to assure both availability and affordability of the terrorism risk using their usual regulatory methods, including pooling by state if necessary. Any plan approved by congress should require state commissioners to ensure that pre-September 11 policy terms are maintained to ensure availability, and should allow Commissioners meaningful authority to assure that rates are affordable.

Further, the states should be asked to assure that the plan enhances security through discounts or other incentives. Congress could set goals for the states in this effort. This requires little, if any new state bureaucracy, because this is what they already do. The plan requires only a handful of people at the federal level to monitor the request for loans, right up to loan documents, et cetera.

We think this plan is fair and the most effective proposed to date, because it protects both the industry and consumers and it makes taxpayers whole, eventually. It is not a handout, it is not a bailout, and perhaps most importantly it can be fully operational on January 1 of next year.

Thank you, Mr. Chairman.

[The statement of Mr. Plunkett follows:]

PREPARED STATEMENT OF ROBERT HUNTER, DIRECTOR OF INSURANCE, CONSUMER FEDERATION OF AMERICA

Good day Mr. Chairman and members of the Committee. I am Bob Hunter, Director of Insurance for the Consumer Federation of America. I previously served as Texas Insurance Commissioner and, of particular relevance to today's subject, as Federal Insurance Administrator under Presidents Ford and Carter.

I served at FIA between 1971 and 1980. My first task was to assist in establishing the Riot Reinsurance Program under the provisions of the Urban Property Protection Act. I strongly encourage you to look at the Riot reinsurance program for guidance in your current important effort for reasons I will cover in the next few minutes.

In the late 1960s, the nation faced great uncertainty from a form of terror from within. There were an awful series of riots in the land. If this were not bad enough for the people in the inner cities who were at the equivalent of what we now call "ground zero," the reinsurers panicked and began to cut off reinsurance protection from the American primary insurance market. The primary insurers, without their layoff arrangements were poised to pull out of the inner cities. Then lenders would have to call mortgages . . . the set up for a true crisis.

Congress, wisely, stepped in, creating the riot reinsurance program. The program adhered to good insurance principles, requiring the government to charge full actuarial rates for the reinsurance and making sure that claims were appropriate for payment.

I was tasked with the job of coming up with actuarially sound rates for the riot reinsurance program. This was about as fearful a job as I ever faced. There was great uncertainty. But actuarial soundness is not defined as precise prices. It relates to procedures such as using the best information available, making reasoned judgments and basically doing your best. We did that, full well expecting to be too high or too low since future events such as riots are hard to predict.

I met with insurers, actuaries from the actuarial societies and other interested parties and came up with prices. Insurers thought they were OK since they bought the reinsurance. The taxpayer was protected and, indeed, profited from the transaction.

Sound insurance principles require proper prices and require adequate supervision of the claims payment process.

CFA SUPPORTS A FEDERAL REINSURANCE PROGRAM FOR TERRORISM

CFA supports a sound program of reinsurance for the terrorism risk underwritten by the federal government.[1] I attach a list of principles CFA developed for Congress to consider when developing the program. Foremost among the principles are that

[1] This testimony relates to property-casualty insurance. The life insurance industry has requested a Commission to study if they need back-up. CFA believes that a Commission is not needed. The life insurance industry should make its case for when they might need help and Congress should call hearings to critique that analysis. CFA looks forward to participating in that separate process.

the insurance industry must be able to purchase affordable reinsurance and that the taxpayer be protected.

INTERIM TERRORISM INSURANCE PROPOSAL

CFA understands that creation of the permanent plan we espouse below might take more time than we have to protect insurers as of January 1, 2002, when most reinsurance runs out. We therefore suggest that an interim, actuarially sound plan be developed.

Simply, we believe that most insurers could withstand at least another event of the magnitude of the September 11th tragedy. So we do not think that the interim plan should cover first dollar losses. CFA proposes that a retention be used for each insurer of 5% of surplus, as of December 31, 2001.

"Terrorism" must be defined for this interim plan and should be determined by a federal official.

If a terrorist attack occurs and an insurer suffers claims greater than the retention amount, the insurer would be eligible for federal low or no interest loans, the term of which would be negotiated up to 30 years. This would spread the cost over time, an important goal. For each insurer, the discounted value of the loan would be limited to an additional 5% of surplus.

Amounts of money loaned in excess of the 5% of surplus by company would be repaid to the U.S. Treasury through a property-casualty insurance industry-wide loan repayment mechanism. This loan repayment would be collected over a number of that are sufficient to minimize the rate impact on consumers (Congress should set the maximum surcharge, perhaps at about 2.5% per year, until the loan is repaid). The surcharge would be collected by the states as a piggyback on their state premium tax mechanism and forwarded on to the U.S. Treasury. This step is needed in order to make sure that individual company balance sheets are not impacted by very large losses due to terrorist activity.

This plan leaves the regulation of insurance fully in state hands. The states should be required to assure availability and affordability of the terrorism risk, using their usual regulatory methods, including pooling by state if necessary. Further, the states should be asked to assure that the plans enhance security through discounts or other incentives. Congress could set goals for the states in this effort. This requires little if any new bureaucracy since much of this sort of work is already part of the state insurance department responsibility.

NEEDED PROTECTIONS FOR THE TAXPAYER

Any longer term plan should protect consumers and taxpayers in the following manner:

> *First,* insurance companies should pay full actuarially sound rates for any reinsurance protection they enjoy. Any plan that requires no premium is not actuarially sound. The insurers need a plan to protect their interests—they do not need a hand out. Insurers should be loathe to set a precedent where inadequate premiums are acceptable when they are paying the premium, if they do not expect consumers to press for inadequately priced home, auto, life and other coverages. When the insurers offer free insurance to us, we will consider free reinsurance for them.
>
> Free insurance is particularly galling in year one of the coverage. Don't forget the insurers made contracts with Americans to cover terrorism fully. These contracts are being entered into even as we speak. So, for a year for policies being written today and for an average of about six months for policies already in force, there would be terrorism coverage even if Congress did nothing. To come in after-the-fact and give away insurance to the industry, which is a very healthy industry[2] even after September 11th, would be foolish.
>
> Actuarial soundness is possible. The taxpayer can be assured that, over time, the program would, at worst, cost the taxpayer nothing. Here is how to do it:
>
> - *Congress should require actuarially sound reinsurance premiums.* That does not mean precision, it means doing the best you can to set a price you think is based on reason.

---

[2] At year-end 2000, the property/casualty industry had surplus of $321 billion and net premium written of $303 billion. The rule of thumb for a very safe industry is a ratio of $1 of surplus for each $2 of net premium written. Thus, the industry had "excess" surplus of $170 Billion. ($321 – $303/2). So, even if the industry has another WTC event, God forbid, they can afford it.

- The plan should include assessments against the industry if terrorism reinsurance claims exceed certain dollar thresholds. During the riot reinsurance days, the industry had to agree to a 2.5% of their total premium assessment provision in the reinsurance contract.
- The plan should have a provision stating that if the taxpayer has paid more into the plan than the premiums and investment of premiums, the premium collection aspects of the plan will stay in effect until the taxpayer is made whole. Just as in the riot reinsurance program, the plan can be self-sustaining over time. Uncertainty will end and the costs shifted to taxpayers during the uncertain times can be recouped as certainty returns.
- The plan should include a wise pay out plan that minimizes taxpayer exposure. The second year of the White House proposal is a good start. That should be the first year of the program. The industry can easily afford a first layer of coverage where they are 100% at risk for tens of billions. I would set it at $35 Billion[3] for year one. The industry could easily afford three such events even today.
- The federal government should have a claims audit role to assure that only claims that meet the definition of terrorism and are within the contractual provisions of the reinsurance policy are paid.

Second, private insurers should not be able to cherry pick against the taxpayer. By "cherry picking" I mean sending bad risks to the federal reinsurance program and keeping good risks for the industry accounts. Thus, all primary insurance companies should be required to participate in the reinsurance program. At the very least, groups of insurers should not be allowed to reinsure one company with "target" risks (*e.g.* the Empire State Building) but not reinsure another company in the group (say, insuring farm risks).

State Consumer Protections Should NOT be Impacted by any Reinsurance Plan

One of the beauties of reinsurance by the federal government is that it is simply a contractual arrangement with the insurer, it does nothing to interfere with the carefully constructed system of state regulation in place.

There Must be a Degree of Bureaucracy to Administer the Program

While it can be minimized, you need staff to develop the contract and administer the claims payment process. You cannot just pay claims. If you do, the taxpayer will be ripped off. You need a small but not insignificant staff (maybe 50?) to do this job.

The setting of the premium charge and the collection of the reinsurance premium requires very few staff (maybe 5?).

Availability and Affordability of Insurance Must Be Assured

The reason for Congress to step into this situation with federal back-up is to make sure that the economy is not frozen by lack of insurance for the terrorism risk. To write a plan that does not do the necessary to assure that insurance is written and the price is reasonable would by foolish.

This means that the plan should include a requirement of continuation of direct provision of terrorism coverage by insurers as part of the "deal" for taxpayer back-up for those risks that meet minimum security standards. Further it means that the rate charged for primary insurance should be correlated with the reinsurance charges so that there is no gouging by insurance companies at this time of national emergency. Congress should not infringe on the ability of state regulators to assure that price gouging for primary insurance does not occur.

CRITIQUE OF INDUSTRY PROPOSAL

The Consumer Federation of America strongly opposes the industry drafted "Insurance Stabilization and Availability Act of 2001." This proposal is a massive overreach that unnecessarily exposes taxpayers to billions of dollars in risk. There are several serious problems with the industry approach:

---

[3] Some have maintained that this is difficult to do since some who suffered loss early would be more exposed that those with later claims. This is a red herring. What you should do, I think, is to allocate the deductible by insurer based on the sorts of risks they have and their surplus level. Then a smaller insurer might be paid even if a terrorist loss was relatively small but in the locus of the exposure that that insurer wrote.

- The bill does not require actuarial soundness. Indeed, insurers would pay nothing for reinsurance for the first year of the program, until the mutual insurance company created under the bill builds up a $10 billion net asset base. Apparently, this free government reinsurance would even cover policies already in force for which insurers are fully at risk today. This is a grossly improper use of taxpayer monies.
- Insurers can "cherry pick" risks since they could opt in or out of the reinsurance program at will. One insurer of a group of companies could be set up to take all of the "bad" risks and buy the reinsurance, effectively adversely selecting against the taxpayer. Further, cherry picking is allowed in that the insurers can decide whether to reinsure personal risks and commercial risks separately.
- The selection of Illinois as the sole regulator of the new federally backed mutual insurer puts consumers at risk. Illinois, unlike most other states, does not control prices. Congress should not interfere with normal insurance protections afforded business and personal consumers. If Congress decides to interfere, a federal agency should be empowered to regulate the insurers, including the rates charged for the reinsured coverages, to assure that no price gouging occurs. (Why enact a terrorism reinsurance program to make insurance affordable and then let insurers charge whatever they want for the coverage?) If one state were to be used to regulate the rates and policies offered (something CFA does not favor), the most advantageous for consumers would be the largest state, California. Studies show that California insurance oversight has been the best in the country over the last decade.
- The bill would cover war events only for workers' compensation. The bill should cover war for all lines of insurance and the reinsurance program should be so constructed.
- The bill waives the application of all federal and state anti-trust laws. This is unnecessary and inappropriate.
- The bill allows territorial differences in pricing, which means that New York City will likely pay much higher rates than other cities, particularly if there is no government review of insurer pricing decisions, as the bill proposes.
- There is no guarantee of affordability or availability of coverage to reasonably secure risks.

We urge you to reject the insurance industry proposal and, instead, use the very successful Urban Property Protection Act of 1969 as the precedent for this program, as reflected in the principles developed by CFA (printed below).

CRITIQUE OF THE WHITE HOUSE PROPOSAL

The White House proposal is flawed for several reasons. First, it is actuarially unsound. The taxpayer should not give away reinsurance.

Second, the first year pay-out plan shows a fundamental misunderstanding of insurance. The 80%/20% split starting at the first dollar of terrorism loss will actually leave the taxpayer exposed to 100% of the risk. This is because the plan will reinsure the reinsurers. So, the primary insurers will reinsure the 20% the taxpayer is not on the hook for with the reinsurers. The reinsurers will then "buy" (for no premium) the 80%/20% cover. This will increase the taxpayer share to 96% (100% − [20% × 20%]). But that is not the end of the reinsurance process. The reinsurers will again reinsure (called "retrocession") with other reinsurers (possibly including the primary carriers themselves). The taxpayer share will then go to 99.2% (100% − [20% × 20% × 20%]). If they reinsure again (there is no limit on how many times the risk can be ping-ponged to lay off risk on the taxpayer) the taxpayer share would be 99.8%. And so on.

This could be corrected by not exposing the taxpayer to private reinsurance payouts.

A better approach would be to change the plan to have a large deductible. As indicated earlier, I think that amount should be $35 billion. Over that, there should be sharing as in year two of the White House plan . . . but no reinsurance should be allowed on private reinsurance claims even in that scenario.

The White House plan also does not guarantee affordability or availability of coverage to reasonably secure risks.

CONCLUSION

Congress can and should back-up the private insurance market with reinsurance for the peril of terrorism. It can and should do it in a wise way that protects the taxpayer and, over time, assures that the taxpayer is reimbursed for the costs of the program so that the cost goes to ratepayers rather than to taxpayers.

CFA looks forward to working with the Congress on this most important effort.

Guiding Principles for Insurance Legislation Related to War and Terrorism

1. CFA supports the concept of federal back-up of the private insurance industry for the perils of war and terrorism. We suggest the riot reinsurance program as a precedent for this backup.
2. Legislation should supplement but not replace other private and public insurance mechanisms where those mechanisms can provide coverage more efficiently. However, all insurers should be required to reinsure against the perils of war and terrorism through the federal government at the outset of the program. In time, as conditions warrant, private reinsurance should be encouraged. To avoid undue taxpayer exposure, however, the program should include a requirement of minimum extended terms for reinsured insurers with claims paid to allow taxpayers to recoup some of the losses.
3. There should be a reasonable coordination and structuring of state and federal regulatory responsibilities with respect to a federal terrorism reinsurance program that achieves the objectives of the program without unnecessarily compromising or preempting state regulatory authority and consumer protections. Necessary preemption of or limits on state regulatory authority should be compensated by requisite federal oversight.
4. There should be an appropriate balance of different private and public interests in the governance of regulatory oversight over the program. Consumers (business and personal), insurers, reinsurers and state regulators of insurance should be on the board of advisors for such program.
5. All records relating to the program, including the records of the reinsured insurance companies should be available for federal audit and, to the maximum extent possible, made public.
6. Rates for the war and terrorism perils charged for the government reinsurance should be actuarially sound and should consider all reasonable factors that can be feasibly measured and supported by theoretical and empirical analysis.
7. The federal government should assure that the cost of terrorism/war coverage charged by reinsured insurance companies to the consumer is actuarially based and correlated in price with the reinsurance offered by the government.
8. The legislation must clearly define "terrorism" and "war" and exclude any coverage beyond those definitions. A top federal official should determine if a specific event falls into either of those definitions.
9. Anti cherry-picking provisions such as the following should be included: Legislation should recognize that many war or terrorism exposures subject the government to potential adverse selection as insurers with less catastrophe risk are less likely to voluntarily purchase coverage, while those with greater risk are more likely to purchase coverage. If legislation were to create a government reinsurance program, the program should encourage the inclusion of both low-risk and high-risk insureds to promote greater risk spreading in a way that does not subject the government to adverse selection.
10. Legislation should promote or encourage coverage that is available to any property that meets reasonable standards of insurability. Federal security requirements should be met within reasonable time periods by insured risks and policed by inspection by reinsured insurers.
11. State residual market mechanisms and other pooling mechanisms for insurance should be allowed to participate in the entity established by legislation to provide war and terrorism insurance, in such a way as to not create incentives for business to be placed in the residual market. To the extent that a risk meets the minimum security requirements, it should be able to get war and terrorism coverage through some source . . . . a residual market if necessary.
12. Jurisdiction over claim settlement practices should remain with the states.
13. Tax law changes should be encouraged to avoid penalties on and encourage the accumulation of reserves for war and terrorism losses.
14. Legislation should encourage loss reduction and hazard mitigation efforts through enhanced security.

Senator NELSON. Thank you, Mr. Plunkett.

We have heard from a multiplicity of interests now, and we want to hear from the industry, Mr. Vagley representing the AIA, and Mr. Nutter representing the Reinsurance Association, so Mr. Vagley, welcome.

STATEMENT OF MR. ROBERT VAGLEY, PRESIDENT, AMERICAN INSURANCE ASSOCIATION

Mr. VAGLEY. Thank you, Mr. Chairman. Thank you for this opportunity to testify before the committee at this critical time in our Nation's deliberations.

Mr. Chairman, the tragic events of September 11, 2001, forever changed our collective understanding of and concern about terrorism. We in our industry lost many valued business colleagues and dear friends on the attacks on the World Trade Center and the Pentagon, and no discussion of this subject should proceed without our heartfelt remembrance of them.

Mr. Chairman, the new post September 11 world is fundamentally different than that which existed before, surely for Americans in general, and very specifically for property casualty insurers and our customers. Current estimates of total insured losses resulting from the September 11 attacks are between $30 to $40 billion at the low end, and $60 to $75 billion at the upper end, although the final number could end up being much higher. It will be by far the most costly insured event in history. The amount of losses from September 11 may well exceed the entire U.S. property casualty insurance industry's net income for the past 3 years.

Notwithstanding the enormity of this loss, the insurance industry is committed to meeting our promises to policyholders affected by the events of September 11. We are paying claims quickly and fully. To date, declared losses total over $20 billion, and we are not seeking any financial assistance to meet these obligations.

Looking ahead, we are very concerned about what will happen if, heaven forbid, there are additional terrorist attacks on our country. The financial capacity of our industry, while sizable, is limited and finite. Unfortunately, the potential harm that terrorists can inflict is both totally unpredictable in frequency and almost infinite in severity. The combination of these two factors, finite capital and infinite risk, makes the risk of terrorism uninsurable.

There is another important aspect to this issue. More than two-thirds of annual reinsurance contracts are renewed each January 1. Reinsurers already have notified primary carriers that they intend to exclude or dramatically scale back terrorism coverage in the reinsurance contracts coming up for renewal. They are not to blame for this. These risks are no more insurable for them than they are for us.

Primary carriers do not have the same flexibility as reinsurers with respect to our own product, because we are subject to tighter regulatory controls. Any terrorism exclusions we might choose to introduce must be approved by individual state insurance departments. If approved, our customers could find themselves bearing 100 percent of the risk associated with terrorism.

Certainly, the repercussions of this are clear. However, if exclusions are denied, insurers will be left to shoulder 100 percent of future terrorist losses which we simply can no longer afford to do. Our only remaining option, one we would prefer not to consider, is to withdraw from certain markets and/or lines of coverage. So in other words, we face a very difficult dilemma.

How can we remain solvent and still serve the real needs of our customers for financial protection against terrorism? We believe the only course of action is enactment of legislation to create a federal financial backstop for losses that result from future terrorist attacks. This backstop could be temporary, but must be enacted before congress recesses for the year in order to avert the market crisis that will occur by January 1.

This is not, repeat, not a bailout for the insurance industry. In fact, the primary beneficiaries of such legislation would be our customers and the U.S. economy. The purpose of the legislation would be to ensure that adequate insurance coverage remains available to American businesses. There are a few ways in which this could be done. One is the British-style reinsurance pool concept which we have advanced. Another is the quota-share approach recently offered by the administration. A third could involve some sort of industry-wide deductible or retention.

We are not wedded to the details of any particular proposal, not even our own, though we do believe it offers the best hope for restoring this market. However, in order for any legislative plan to be successful in averting the looming economic crisis, it must be drafted in a way that improves predictability, stabilizes the market, and preserves insurer solvency.

We understand that in all likelihood any new risk-sharing mechanism for terrorism coverage will include some significant retention of future losses by private insurers. On that point, I would like to note that the more risk insurers are required to retain, the less stability there will be in the marketplace, and the higher the retention, the higher premiums will have to be.

Mr. Chairman, terrorism has become uninsurable in the private marketplace as currently structured. Appreciating that an immediate stopgap solution may be somewhat imperfect, we expect that dislocations will still occur as insurers may cautiously reenter the marketplace. It is our hope that, with time and experience, we will be able to craft longer term, more complete solutions that avoid such disruptions.

In the absence of federal legislation to prevent the complete collapse of the commercial insurance market, entire sectors of the U.S. economy could be left wholly exposed and unable to continue the normal course of business. I respectfully urge you to act quickly and decisively to ensure that all businesses are able to obtain much-needed protection against future losses.

Thank you for your attention, and I look forward to responding to your questions, Mr. Chairman.

[The statement of Mr. Vagley follows:]

PREPARED STATEMENT OF ROBERT E. VAGLEY, PRESIDENT, AMERICAN INSURANCE ASSOCIATION

Chairman Hollings, Ranking Minority Member McCain, Subcommittee Chairman Dorgan and other members of the Committee, my name is Robert E. Vagley, and I am president of the American Insurance Association, the leading property and casualty insurance trade organization in the United States, representing more than 410 insurers that write over $87 billion in premiums each year. AIA member companies offer all types of property and casualty insurance, including those most impacted by the horrific events of September 11: commercial liability, commercial property, and workers' compensation. Before I begin my formal remarks, I would like to thank you for holding this important hearing this morning and for this opportunity to testify before the Commerce Committee at this crucial time.

The tragic events of September 11, 2001, forever changed our collective understanding of, and concern about, terrorism on our own shores. The scope and nature of those attacks were unprecedented in world history. None of us—neither private nor public sector interests—had made accommodations for this type of occurrence, because such things were simply beyond our conception. Unfortunately, we are now presented with a new view of the very real risks and potentially infinite costs associated with terrorist acts. The new, post-September 11 world in which we find ourselves is fundamentally different than that which existed before, for Americans in general, and very specifically for property/casualty insurers and our customers.

Today, I would like to address two topics. First, I would like to briefly describe how our industry has responded to the tragic events of September 11. Then, I would like to share our thoughts on how we can make certain that insurers are able to continue meeting the expectations and future needs of our policyholders with respect to terrorism and the wide range of other risks which we insure.

Current estimates of total insured losses resulting from the September 11 attacks stand at between $30 billion and $60 billion, although the final number will not be known for some time, and could end up being much higher. This makes the September 11 attacks, by far, the most costly insured event in history. Although no natural disaster or man-made catastrophe even comes close, for the sake of some reference, I would note that Hurricane Andrew, which devastated south Florida in 1992, caused approximately $19 billion in insured losses, perhaps half to one third of the September 11 losses. Put another way, the September 11 losses will exceed the entire property/casualty industry's net income for the past three years (1999, 2000, and 2001). On that single day, three years of industry profits, including investment income, were wiped out.

I want to be very clear about our response to the horrific attack on the World Trade Center. Notwithstanding the enormity of this loss, the insurance industry has been publicly and steadfastly committed to meeting our promises to policyholders affected by the events of September 11. We have not attempted to invoke war exclusions, despite the militaristic nature of, and rhetoric surrounding, the attacks. We are paying our claims quickly and fully. We have received claims in excess of $20 billion to date. And, unlike other industries who were directly affected by the attacks, we are not asking for any financial assistance from legislators or regulators to meet our obligations.

Recognizing that the American people and our economy will recover and move onward, we also are looking ahead. Although the property/casualty insurance industry can deal with the incredible losses from September 11, we are very concerned about what will happen if there are additional, large-scale terrorist attacks in the future. It is critical that you as public policymakers share our recognition that terrorism currently presents core challenges to the insurance market that we cannot meet.

The financial capacity of our industry, while sizable, is limited. Unfortunately, the potential harm that terrorists can inflict is both totally unpredictable in frequency and unlimited in severity. As Warren Buffet, CEO of Berkshire-Hathaway, recently stated, "Terrorism today is not at all like terrorism 25 years ago. And now you've got something where the nature of the risk, the power to inflict damage, has gone up a factor of—who knows what—10, 50 . . . you can't price for that." Put simply, that which is not quantifiable is not insurable in the traditional sense.

As you probably are aware, more than two-thirds of annual reinsurance contracts—agreements by which primary insurance companies purchase their own insurance to adequately spread the risk of large-scale losses—are renewed each January 1. Reinsurers already have notified primary carriers that they intend to exclude or dramatically scale back terrorism coverage in the reinsurance contracts coming up for renewal. Although the primary insurance sector of the industry is adversely affected by such decisions, we recognize that this may well be the reinsurers' only way to protect their own solvency.

Primary carriers, however, do not have the same flexibility as reinsurers with respect to our own products because we are subject to tighter regulatory controls. Any terrorism exclusions we might choose to introduce must be approved by individual state insurance departments. If approved, our customers could find themselves bearing 100 percent of the risks associated with terrorism. Certainly, the repercussions of this are clear. However, if exclusions were not approved, primary insurers would be left to shoulder 100 percent of future terrorist losses, which we simply cannot afford to do. Our only remaining option—one we would prefer not to consider—would be to simply withdraw from certain markets, and/or lines of coverage.

So we face a very difficult challenge: how can we remain solvent, and still serve the real needs of our customers for financial protection against terrorism? I am proud to say that insurers are working hard with you and your colleagues in the House, and with the Bush Administration, to come up with a public policy solution that will allow us to continue providing this much-needed coverage to our policyholders.

We believe that the only course of action is immediate enactment of legislation to create a federal financial backstop for losses that result from future terrorist attacks. This backstop could be temporary, existing only for as long as it is needed. The legislation must be enacted before Congress recesses for the year, since so many reinsurance contracts which cover this risk will expire on January 1.

The legislation we are seeking is not, repeat *not,* a "bailout" for the insurance industry. In fact, the primary beneficiaries of such legislation would be our customers, and the U.S. economy. Ultimately, the costs of risk must be borne by the policyholders who seek protection through insurance. Given the unprecedented nature of the terrorism threat, the best way for this to be done is through a public/private partnership that allows us to service the coverage needs of our policyholders while remaining financially strong enough to pay all potential claims, whether from terrorism acts or the other ordinary and extraordinary events that affect our business.

The goal of needed legislation is to ensure that adequate insurance coverage remains available to American businesses. Federal Reserve Chairman Alan Greenspan recognized this when he testified before Congress last week, coming to what he termed the "very unusual conclusion that the viability of free markets may, on occasion, when you are dealing with a degree of violence, require that the costs of insurance are basically reinsured by the taxpayer, as indeed they are, for example, in Great Britain and in Israel and in other countries which have run into problems quite similar to ours."

There are a number of ways in which this could be done. One is the British-style reinsurance pool concept, and another is the quota share approach recently suggested by the Administration. A third would involve some sort of industry-wide deductible or retention. We are not wedded to the details of any particular proposal; not even our own. However, in order for any legislative plan to be successful in averting the looming economic crisis, it must be drafted in a way that improves predictability, stabilizes the market, and preserves insurer solvency.

No proposal can make the risk of terrorism go away, nor can it make the cost of insurance against terrorism risk go away. However, the right legislation can provide a way for the public and private sectors, on a short-term basis, to co-manage this risk—a risk whose dimensions changed fundamentally and exponentially on September 11.

What must be in the legislation from our perspective to make it workable? First, rather than 51 possible separate definitions of "terrorist act," there must be a uniform national definition that will constitute the terrorism coverage provided by insurance policies all across America. A broad national definition of terrorism is essential to avoid non-concurrence of coverages among primary insurers, reinsurers and the federal backstop. Such uniformity cannot be achieved if states retain the authority to approve or disapprove policy forms in this narrow area.

Second, insurers must be able to quickly include the price for terrorism coverage in their insurance policies, rather than be required to go to every state insurance regulator and seek that regulator's approval for the terrorism rate in every property/casualty line. Even with a federal terrorism reinsurance program that provides a partial backstop, individual insurers' retention for terrorism risk will be expensive, given the huge uncertainties and potentially large losses we collectively face as a nation. States cannot take the attitude that "terrorism can't happen in our particular backyard," and therefore suppress rates. Mindful of the general prerogatives of state insurance regulators in the rate-setting arena, there must be language in place that preserves rate review by the appropriate state regulator, but does not subject the rates to any review or approval prior to or in connection with the timely introduction of those rates into the marketplace.

Third, we recognize that any federal terrorism reinsurance program will include a number of important details with respect to the mechanics of reimbursement and other issues. These details must be drafted and implemented in a way that is workable for insurance companies and our regulators.

We understand that, in all likelihood, any new risk sharing mechanism for terrorism coverage will include some significant retention of future losses by private insurers. On that point, I would like to note that the more risk insurers are forced to retain, the less stability there will be in the marketplace. Also, the higher the retention, the higher prices will have to be.

Terrorism has become uninsurable in the private marketplace as currently structured. Period. Appreciating that an immediate, stopgap solution may be somewhat imperfect, we expect that dislocations will still occur as insurers cautiously re-enter the marketplace. It is our hope that, with time and experience, we will be able to craft longer-term, more complete solutions that avoid such disruptions.

In the absence of federal legislation to prevent the complete collapse of the commercial insurance market, entire sectors of the U.S. economy could be left wholly exposed and unable to continue the normal course of business. I urge you to act quickly and decisively to ensure that all businesses are able to obtain much-needed protection against future losses.

I thank you for your attention and look forward to responding to your questions.

Senator NELSON. Thank you, Mr. Vagley. Mr. Nutter.

STATEMENT OF MR. FRANKLIN NUTTER, PRESIDENT, REINSURANCE ASSOCIATION OF AMERICA

Mr. NUTTER. Thank you very much. I am mindful of the hour, and my position on the panel.

Senator NELSON. You go ahead, and you take the allotted time, and then we are going to get into a good discussion here.

Mr. NUTTER. I appreciate that.

The Reinsurance Association of America represents domestic U.S. reinsurance companies. Reinsurance is effectively the insurance of insurance companies. It is commonly associated with natural disasters, hurricanes and earthquakes. The chairman is well aware of the role that insurance and reinsurance has played in dealing with that. As compared to the primary insurance market, some estimates are that the losses associated with the events of September 11 will fall 60 percent in the reinsurance market. This shows the role that reinsurance plays in dealing with catastrophic events.

I will not repeat, but certainly would associate with the comments that Bob Vagley made about what this industry is seeking. We are certainly seeking no compensation, no program, no financial assistance for the events of September 11. What I would like to comment on are various references that have been made to the asset base or the capital base of the industry and how it relates to this issue. No insurance or reinsurance premiums were collected for the acts of terrorism that occurred on September 11. All of the losses will be paid out of the capital account of the industry.

As has been mentioned, I think by you, Mr. Chairman, the industry's capital base is about $300 billion, but these losses fall not evenly across that capital base, but fall mostly on commercial insurers and reinsurers. That capital base really falls to about $125 or $126 billion for those companies that will bear the greatest portion of this loss. Some estimates are the capital base is lower than that.

That capital base clearly can fund the September 11 losses, and it will fund them, but the companies in the industry will look at these losses and reevaluate a variety of underwriting principles. Certainly with respect to the size, scope, and frequency of these kinds of insured losses, greater capital allocation will be necessary. Risk-based standards applied by insurance commissioners are likely to incorporate terrorism risks that they have not previously applied. Even the notion of the correlation of risk that we did not contemplate before but that we now see in an act of terrorism will have to be rethought.

The industry cannot absorb losses of this nature with any frequency. The potential unlimited size of the exposure, the frequency of the exposure, and the scale make it very difficult. As Mr. Vagley has said, it is probably an uninsurable risk. We have then to look to other ways of dealing with this. Insurance, as has been said by many witnesses, is the grease that operates to lubricate the American economy. We are here to find ways to continue to provide insurance and reinsurance to our clients.

The best way is that the federal government should be an insurer of last resort, a reinsurer, if you will. We also are not currently wedded to any specific approach, but we do recognize the urgency of this problem. As has been mentioned, many reinsurance contracts do renew at year end, and frankly, the reinsurance community is looking to the Congress to take action. That will have a direct bearing and significant bearing on what they do with respect to providing coverage for terrorist acts.

We would like to work with the committee, and certainly work with the congress in finding solutions. We do think that it is important that in any such legislation that provides that the federal government is a reinsurer of last resort, that some clear definition of terrorism is made, some establishment of a framework for the regulation of rates at the State level is made, and the basis upon which insurers and reinsurers will retain risk on their own account should be clarified.

With that, Mr. Chairman, I will close and welcome any questions from the committee.

[The statement of Mr. Nutter follows:]

PREPARED STATEMENT OF FRANKLIN W. NUTTER, PRESIDENT, REINSURANCE ASSOCIATION OF AMERICA

The Reinsurance Association of America represents U.S. domestic reinsurers, which collectively underwrite more than 70 percent of the U.S. reinsurance market. Reinsurance is the insurance of insurance companies. It is the financial mechanism by which insurers spread the risk of loss throughout the world's capital markets. One of the most frequently used purposes of reinsurance is to absorb losses from catastrophic events such as hurricanes, earthquakes, and in the case of September 11, acts of terrorism. Some have estimated that 60 percent of the losses paid by our industry from the events of September 11, will be paid by reinsurers.

The U.S. insurance and reinsurance industry will be able to meet its policy and contract obligations and pay the losses arising out of the September 11 terrorist attacks. Insurers and reinsurers do not need financial assistance from the federal government for those losses, and they aren't asking for any.

The terrorist attacks of September 11, 2001 resulted in unprecedented losses of life, personal injury and property damage. It is difficult to estimate the total injured losses that the U.S. property and casualty insurance and reinsurance industry will ultimately pay as a result of those terrorist attacks. In addition to the normal problems involved in estimating large or catastrophic losses, in this case there may be liability issues that may take time to fully resolve.

Some recent analysts' reports have suggested that $30 billion to $40 billion is a reasonable range of estimated total insured losses (property, casualty, life and health) from the September 1 terrorist attacks. Some analysts have even suggested that the total insured losses could exceed the range of numbers I just mentioned. Put in perspective, the insured losses from the terrorist acts of September 11 could exceed the combined insured losses from the last five major natural catastrophes (hurricanes Andrew and Hugo, the Northridge, California and Kobe, Japan earthquakes and European windstorms Lothar and Martin).

Before September 11, the threat of terrorism within our borders seemed remote. Because of that, no insurance or reinsurance premiums were collected for terrorism coverage, and no assets or reserves were allocated to terrorism exposures. The industry did not underwrite for the risk of terrorism. That means that the September 11 terrorism losses must be paid from the industry's capital account. The total capital and surplus of the U.S. property and casualty insurance and reinsurance industry at June 30, 2001—including both personal lines and commercial lines writers—

was $298 billion. That figure includes $26.6 billion of capital in separately capitalized U.S. domestic professional reinsurers.

That total industry capital consists of required regulatory risk-based capital, as well as the additional capital need to support operating and investment risks and to meet the reasonable expectations of policyholders and claimants, rating agencies, stockholders and others.

The exposure to loss from the September 11 terrorist attacks is not spread evenly across the total insurance industry capital base. The great bulk of those losses will fall on the capital base of the commercial lines insurers and reinsurers.

After subtracting personal lines capital, the Berkshire Hathaway capital that isn't allocated to the affected lines, and the pre-September 11 third quarter declines in common stock values—the affected property and casualty commercial lines insurers and reinsurers (U.S. and non-U.S.) had a September 10 estimated combined total capital base of $126 billion. Tillinghast, in a just-released study for the American Insurance Association, noted that the September 11 losses might rest on an even smaller capital base—perhaps $80 billion to $100 billion.

Several conclusions can be drawn from this:

> First, the commercial lines capital base can obviously fund a total September 11 insured loss of $25 billion to $40 billion—or an even larger loss from that event.
>
> Second, many actuarial and underwriting principles and practices will have to change. While not a complete list, here are five things that will change:
>
> - We will have new and different notions about the size, shape and trends of insured losses and the required risk loads.
> - Most lines of business will require a greater capital allocation.
> - Risk-based capital standards will be revised by regulators and rating agencies to incorporate terrorism risk.
> - The cost of capital for the insurance business will, other things being equal, go up.
> - We need to rethink risk diversification or its opposite, the correlation of risk.
>
> Third, the commercial lines capital base cannot absorb another sizable terrorist event without seriously compromising the ability of the property and casualty commercial lines industry to meet its commitments for losses arising from other underwriting and balance sheet risks.

The simple fact is that, on its own, the U.S. insurance and reinsurance industry can't afford to take on the potentially unlimited exposure to loss arising from insuring against terrorist acts. No one at present can reasonably predict either the number, scale or frequency of future terrorist attacks we might face before our war on terrorism is won.

We support and applaud the steps that the federal government is taking to combat terrorism. But until those efforts have borne the fruit of significant reduction in the potential for terrorist attacks, it is close to impossible for many insurers and reinsurers to responsibly underwrite or assume terrorism risk. We simply can't evaluate the frequency and severity of terrorism losses using traditional underwriting and actuarial techniques. There are no models that would let us price the risk with confidence.

That is why as an industry we need to explore alternative ways to cover losses arising from terrorism.

The September 24, 2001 edition of *The Wall Street Journal* featured this quote from Warren Buffet, Berkshire Hathaway's chairman:

> I think in the future, the government is going to have to be the ultimate insurer for acts of terrorism. . . . An industry with very large, but finite, resources is not equipped to handle infinite losses.

In some very important ways, insurance is the grease that lubricates the American economic machine. Insurance and reinsurance coverage for terrorism risks is necessary for our economic recovery—so that lenders will lend, and builders will build, and employers will hire.

Going forward, we need to find a way to provide insurance against terrorist acts that assures both the continued financial viability of the U.S. insurance and reinsurance industry, and the continued availability and affordability of the wide range of products and services provided.

In a rare—if not unique—show of unity, the property and casualty insurance and reinsurance industries universally agree that the best way to do that is to have the federal government act as the "reinsurer of last resort" for terrorism insurance and reinsurance coverage, similar to the plan used in the United Kingdom.

Federal Reserve Chairman Alan Greenspan appears to agree. On October 17, 2001, he said:

> What hostile environments do is induce people to withdraw, to disengage, to pull back. It's quite conceivable you could get a level of general hostility that would make viable market functioning very difficult . . . I can conceive of situations [where] the premiums that would be necessary to enable a private insurance company to insure against all those risks and still get a rate of return on their capital would be so large as to inhibit people from actually taking out that insurance. . . .
>
> Therefore you're led to what is an unusual conclusion that the viability of free markets on unusual occasions, when you are dealing with violence . . . [that it is necessary that] the costs of insurance are reinsured by the taxpayers . . .
>
> Free markets and government reinsurance, in this very unusual circumstance they are indeed compatible . . .
>
> (*Source: Bloomberg*)

It is increasingly clear that state regulators, the Administration, members of Congress, and a broad swath of Americans and American businesses also agree that we need a solution.

All of these interests may not currently agree on the exact way to structure that federal insurer role—we've all heard the several proposals that have been advanced. But there is nearly universal agreement on the fact that this is a significant and urgent problem that needs to be solved before Congress recesses.

While the size and scale of the September 11 terrorist attacks are unprecedented, there are precedents for government involvement—here and abroad—in the solution of temporary insurance market disruptions. The federal government ran an insurance program during World War II. FAIR plans were developed to deal with insurance scarcity in the wake of the 1960's urban riots. More recently, the United Kingdom and other countries have developed government-backed solutions to terrorism insurance.

When the need for these kinds of programs abates, they should be terminated.

We're eager to work with this Committee, other members of Congress, the Administration, state insurance regulators, and others to find a solution that makes sense for the country and for the faltering economy, which badly needs an injection of confidence. The solution must also make sense for policyholders and claimants, for the insurance industry and its regulators, and for you. Insurance is, after all, a critical part of the central nervous system of this economy and this society.

We are not looking for any financial assistance for the insured losses flowing from the tragic events of September 11. We are looking for a way forward to serve our clients by protecting against the financial consequences from acts of terrorism, fulfill our role in the economy, and to protect our solvency.

We believe that a public private partnership premised upon the federal government as a reinsurer of last resort provides the best approach. Legislation creating such a mechanism should clearly define terrorism for this purpose, should establish a framework for regulation of rates for state insurance commissioners and provide the basis upon which insurers retain risk on their own account.

Insurers believe that acts of terrorism have become uninsurable in the traditional sense. Only a public/private partnership, even one that is transitory in nature can address this problem.

I'm grateful for the opportunity to speak to you today, and would be pleased to answer any questions you may have.

Senator NELSON. Thank you all for excellent presentations. I thought I was escaping from the state level of insurance regulation to the high councils and marble corridors of the federal government, where I would not be facing the question of insurance, and yet here we are.

Senator Boxer has a commitment then she has to leave. You are recognized.

Senator BOXER. Thank you so much, and I just want to say how lucky we are to have you here, because this is in many ways a complicated issue, although I sense it is being made a little bit more complicated than it should be made, but we will see.

First, I want to compliment the insurance industry, because I want you to know, when I heard you say we are going to cover these losses, we are okay, we are healthy, we are strong, I felt really good about that, and I felt that it did add a certain level of calm and peace to people who were suffering so much that this was one less thing they had to deal with, so I do want to say that I am appreciative of that, and I am glad of that, and you did not come running here for September 11.

I want to talk about the future, because I do not think it should be all that confusing, and here is what I am going to do. I want to explain what we do in California vis a vis earthquakes, and then what I would love to do, because I do not want to take the time of my chair today, is if you would promise me to explain what you like about this plan, what would not work, how you would change it, or if you just think the whole thing does not apply. But rather than go through it as a dialogue, I would prefer to speak first, and then I will leave and leave the rest to my colleague from Florida.

Here is what happened after the horrible Northridge, California earthquake in 1994. Insurance companies determined that the premiums they had been charging for earthquake coverage were inadequate. Furthermore, the companies did not know how to set an actuarially sound price, which is something we are discussing here today. Insurance companies attempted to stop selling insurance against earthquake damage, and I can tell you that really created havoc in our state. People were just so upset, Mr. Chairman. Here they had this earthquake, and now they were going to lose all future coverage.

The state said, unh-unh, you cannot do that and still function in the state. You are going to have to figure out a way to do this. So there were negotiations between the legislature and the Governor, the insurance companies, and after the negotiations, insurers were permitted to exclude earthquake coverage from their property casualty policies if insurance companies representing at least 70 percent of the market agreed to participate in the California Earthquake Authority, so this California Earthquake Authority was set up to participate. It meant agreeing to an initial assessment totaling $717 million, plus two additional assessments of $2.1 billion and $1.4 billion after certain levels of earthquake-related losses occurred. Thus, potential earthquake authority losses are to be funded by multilayered financing arrangements involving insurer contributions, premiums, conventional reinsurance, and preestablished debt financing.

Now, in early 2000, these layers totaled about $7 billion. Now, the state of California does not put any money into this, and in the event all the authority funds are expended, claim payments would be prorated. The Earthquake Authority currently provides all of the earthquake insurance available in the state.

Now, I do not think this goes far enough. I think the federal government should do more, et cetera, et cetera, but what I would like—and I am not to get into it now—if you could critique the ideas of this proposal, because it does appear to be working.

In closing, Mr. Chairman, let me say this. I want to help, but I cannot sit by and watch the taxpayers be taken advantage of. I cannot. I will not. That is not why I am here. Other people may be able to, but I cannot, so I am really hoping that we come up with a plan, all of us, that everybody feels good about, that yes, the taxpayers will be there as a last resort, not first resort, that we will be there to help, and I think that—the comments of Mr. Keating and Mr. Moss and Mr. Plunkett reflect where I am coming from on this.

I think we can do what we have to do, Mr. Chairman, but we need to be mindful that we do not want to interfere too much. I mean, after all, that is what we are told all along. You do not want to set up an artificial situation here, and I was taken by what Mr. Moss said. I think it was Mr. Moss who said, you do not want to take incentives away.

For example, if you just have the insurers feel, that they do not have to worry about this any more and only have a little bit of liability, and believe that Uncle Sam has most of it, and then somebody does not really insure their property. Let us say it gets to the point where insurance companies will be telling their people, we think you ought to have 24-hour security guard, and somebody does not do it, and as a result some damage is done; we have lost our guard because we do not have those financial incentives.

I sense that maybe we were a little more critical on this committee than other committees have been so far. So I hope, as a result of this hearing that we can get to the table and work with you. I hope we can. We need to do something. I think we have some models we can follow.

And again, Mr. Chairman, I am really glad you are here now, because you are going to be one of my leaders on this, that is for sure.

Thank you.

Senator NELSON. Thank you, Senator Boxer.

Well, we have quite a number of proposals on the table. We have the administration's plan, we have the industry's plan, we have the National Taxpayers Union plan, we have the Consumer Federation of America's plan. I would like the National Association of Insurance Commissioner's commentary on what would you like to see the Congress pass to address the terrorism insurance?

Ms. KOKEN. Senator Nelson, it is a pleasure to be here, particularly with you chairing the meeting. The NAIC has developed guiding principles that we think are important, but we have not at this point endorsed any one particular program. We believe that certain aspects are critical. We believe in a sunset, and that it is important that this does not destroy the competitive marketplace, which we think functions best.

At the same time, we do have concerns about the affordability and the availability, but we believe that the state system needs to be kept an important part of whatever the solution is. The system is in place, and we believe that we are very concerned about not only the claims-paying ability of the companies and their ability to follow through with paying claims, and the availability to consumers, but also the very important factor of solvency monitoring, which is something that the state system works very hard at doing, and so we would like to be part of any process.

Senator NELSON. So in that regard, let me ask Mr. Nutter and Mr. Vagley, as I understand your proposal, it basically would take to the federal level a lot of the functions that are now done at the state level that Ms. Koken says the NAIC would oppose. Would you comment on that?

Mr. VAGLEY. Yes, I would say that is not a fair characterization of our proposal, Mr. Chairman. Our proposal really in many respects met the design that you and Senator Boxer described. It was based on the British model, and on models that other countries have adopted when they unfortunately experienced terrorism at home. And the U.K. developed a model called Pool Re, which we in effect sought to emulate by developing our own proposal. It would create a private mutual insurance company that in fact would purchase reinsurance from the federal government. I suspect that proposal was too complicated to consider at this late hour, given the emergence of January 1 and the economic dislocations that might occur then, but it did in many respects meet the goal that you had outlined.

I think except for two narrow areas, Mr. Chairman, we would not propose removing or eliminating the State regulatory body for its assigned mission. The only areas we have called attention to, and I believe these areas have met with concurrence from the state regulatory community, although Ms. Koken certainly is more capable to speak to that than I, one had to do with the definition of terrorism, whatever the definition is, if it is narrow, if it is broad, it should be identical in all policies and all states,and we should not be confused, and policyholders should not be confused by 51 or more different definitions of terrorism.

Then the other area really had to do with pricing the product, Mr. Chairman. We just did not want to be caught up in product approval regimes where we have pending actions before state regulatory bodies for months and years while the risk of terrorism continued.

Senator NELSON. And in fact, then, what Ms. Koken was talking about, that state insurance regulators ought to stay in control of the financial wherewithal of the companies as well as what the rates are. In your proposal, that is done by the federal government, as I understand it. The Treasury Department would oversee the pool, the government reinsurance pool. You would sell terrorism policies from that pool, and the pool would be responsible for paying the terrorism claims, and the premiums collected by the pool would be set by whom?

Mr. VAGLEY. By the federal government in the proposal you are describing, Mr. Chairman, and I should have added, I should have footnoted my comment that there have been several evolutions of that proposal over time, and they seem to be morphing in whatever is the current discussion. With respect to the current debate, the only areas of state authority that would be affected, as I understand it, would be the definition of terrorism, and there the goal would be consistency, and with respect to pricing the product, and that matter would be left to the states, but basically on a final use approach with a general standard of rates not being inadequate, unfairly discriminatory, or excessive.

Senator NELSON. I take it your latest proposal is that the terrorism insurance would be determined by the federal government, in this case the Treasury Department or some derivative thereof, and the insurance premiums would be determined by that agency as well.

Mr. VAGLEY. Again, I guess I should emphasize our proposal has been overtaken by time.

Senator NELSON. Is that your proposal?

Mr. VAGLEY. That was the proposal that we advanced several weeks ago, I think in the several evolutionary stages of the debate. That proposal seems to have little, if any, political traction.

Senator NELSON. Well, what are you advocating now?

Mr. VAGLEY. As I indicated in my testimony, Mr. Chairman, we are advocating anything, any proposal—we are not wedded to any particular proposal—any proposal that will allow the industry to ease its way back into underwriting this product, and that will provide some stability in the commercial insurance marketplace, and there are several proposals on the table, and obviously Congress is free to consider all of them on its own.

Mr. NUTTER. Mr. Chairman, if I could just supplement that. Obviously you are looking at references to an AIA proposal of some weeks ago. As Insurance Commissioner, you are probably familiar that it is not uncommon for the industry to come forward with four or five very good ideas, but in competition with each other. About 10 days ago, we worked with the AIA and the other trade associations in the industry to come up with a consensus proposal that is state-based. A pool with state rate regulation as described by Mr. Vagley, a single definition of terrorism at the federal level. It really has a much more state-based approach than what you are describing. If we need to provide to the committee a more current approach that represents a consensus among the industry's trades, we will do so.

Senator NELSON. Well, one of the ideas that is being proffered now is that the first dollar loss due to terrorism would not be borne jointly by the insurance industry and the federal government, but rather up to a certain level would be borne by the insurance industry. Is that something that you would favorably consider?

Mr. VAGLEY. I think that certainly is a proposal that is on the table, Mr. Chairman, and may be the reigning proposal as of today. Currently I think our focus is restoring responsibility to the marketplace. I would say to those developing those proposals there are better alternatives, including the pool proposal we advanced, and the quota share proposal that the administration advanced.

Simply in terms of allowing underwriters to get their arms around the risk, I think a retention proposal suffers from the significant disability that the Secretary pointed out, which is the misfortune for those who are under the deductible. I mean, who insures this year's tower, when in fact the total loss on that tower might be whatever its total value is. We are operating in a new risk paradigm. No one in our industry, or I dare say our country—perhaps some—could have foreseen how our assessment of risk would change from September 10 to September 11.

Our underwriters used to look at a building like the World Trade Center, and it would be valued in total for $3 or $4 billion, and they would assume that the probable maximum loss in that building, insuring it through fire or other disaster, would be $300 or $400 million. With deep respect to those who were lost in that building, I think if it were reconstructed, underwriters would look at a $4 billion building and say, probably maximum loss is $4 billion.

Senator NELSON. Now, that is what the Secretary was talking about, but that is a 100-percent risk premium, and that is just simply not the business of insurance. You cannot go and charge a $4 billion insurance premium to cover a $4 billion building.

Mr. VAGLEY. That is exactly right. That is why we are here.

Senator NELSON. Well, let me have you critique Mr. Plunkett's plan, the Consumer Federation of America's plan.

Mr. VAGLEY. As I understand Mr. Plunkett's plan, and there was possibly more detail in there that I could comprehend——

Senator NELSON. It was the same one offered last week by Bob Hunter, the Consumer Federation.

Mr. VAGLEY. Assuming that, I think that it is in effect a loan program, and once you reach a certain threshold of pain on a company by company basis, that company would have some access to some lending authority, presumably the lending authority of the federal government. Well, that is an interesting concept, but it does not change the risk paradigm for an underwriter. The underwriter has still got to assume that that company is eating all of the loss.

Whether it pays for that loss out of its capital account or through borrowed funds, those funds may be repaid, so I think the plan fails, because it does not change the risk paradigm. Therefore it does nothing, and we are better off without a program like that, because it would raise expectations that we cannot meet.

Senator NELSON. So you would like to basically—you would rather shift the terrorism risk to a pool of all insurance companies together, and the cost for that pool you might want to consider shared with the federal government, and that any of the costs of that pool to you, the industry, you would pass on to the consumers.

Mr. VAGLEY. Actually, Mr. Chairman, the pool concept that we developed would have operated as a mutual insurance company. The industry would have been able companies like the ones I represent, would have been able to come in and negotiate with this mutual insurance company that would have been called Homeland Security, or Pool Re, or something like that, and basically spread its risk, mutualize its risk, as Secretary O'Neill said, throughout the rest of the industry.

Senator NELSON. That means you put the risk back on the policyholders.

Mr. VAGLEY. No. What that means is, you spread that risk throughout the entire industry, so instead of an underwriter bearing 100 percent of the risk, the underwriter might cede off 95 percent of that risk and retain 5 percent of it, and that is a much more digestible economic proposition than hanging on to 100 percent of the Sears Tower.

Senator NELSON. Right, and your example, if you take 5 percent of the risk and you have 95 percent of the risk in the pool, that then is shared by the entire consortium that is participating in that pool.

Mr. VAGLEY. That is correct, and for that privilege the ceding company would pay a reinsurance fee to the pool.

Senator NELSON. And of course, who pays? The consumer pays in the end, which is what the consumer is going to pay in the end whether they be labeled taxpayer or insurance consumer.

Mr. VAGLEY. Well, if the consumer is a policyholder, the policyholder pays for insurance, that is right.

Senator NELSON. Do you think the industry is going to approach this whole thing, that the whole thing is a 100-percent risk?

Mr. VAGLEY. No. I think the industry——

Senator NELSON. What is actuarially sound in determining a premium.

Mr. VAGLEY. Mr. Chairman, I will tell you that there is no actuarially sound experience that we have. Six weeks after September 11. Now, 2 years from now, or 3 years from now, with the benefit of hindsight and some experience, I would think our actuaries would be better suited to answer that question, but our risk paradigm changed in the 24 hours between September 10 and September 11. Our industry absorbed $40 to $60, $70 billion worth of losses on no premium paid because we honestly did not believe on September 11 that we could have conceived a risk of this nature, and yet we did, and so our risk paradigm has changed, and so we need to reflect that in our own experience, and frankly that analysis has not settled down yet.

Senator NELSON. Nor will it for some number of years, and just on that score, let me ask you, then, how would, in this limited new experience in this strange new world, how would you come up with a pool concept whereby the insurance companies would have 5 percent and the pool would have 95 percent?

Mr. VAGLEY. Well, it actually functions that way, Mr. Chairman. The British experience is illustrative. The British government created a mechanism after the IRA attacks, I believe, in the early nineties. The United Kingdom has never spent a pound to pay back to the insurance industry. That pool has been a self-funding mechanism, and the insurance process will work so long as that risk can be spread. That is why insurance companies go to reinsurance companies to insure themselves. That is why individuals come to us to insure themselves, so that that risk need not be borne by them, so it can be spread through the entire mechanism. That is how the pool concept would have worked.

Senator NELSON. Mr. Nutter, you have been trying to speak.

Mr. NUTTER. I wanted to add a point of clarification. The pool concept that Bob is describing is not unlike the transformer mechanism that was the Florida hurricane fund, really a mechanism by which all companies operating in that case in the Florida market could pool their risk that none of them had such a concentration of risk that it made it threatening to their solvency, or that would in fact affect the rates of individual consumers.

The other thing that has not been said that needs to be said, because it was asked several times of the Secretary, is that our concept had the pool paying the federal government for the reinsurance level that it provided so we looked at this on what we believed to be sound economic grounds so that the consumer, yes, paid for his insurance, but the pool then really moderated the effect of that, and then the pool paid for the cost of reinsurance the federal government provided.

Senator NELSON. By the way, is this one of the few times the reinsurance industry and the insurance industry have been on the same page?

Mr. VAGLEY. It is unusual.

Senator NELSON. Mr. Nutter, I think you were referring to the Florida Windstorm Insurance Foundation when you were referring to the hurricane fund. Let us make sure instead of the Florida hurricane catastrophic fund you were referring to the Windstorm Association.

Mr. NUTTER. I was referring to the Windstorm Association, and of course the role the hurricane fund plays in providing reinsurance through a quasi-governmental organization. This would be different from what we proposed, which is entirely a private sector mechanism subject to state regulation.

Senator NELSON. And having raised that, I want the record to reflect that originally that pool in Florida was created as a consortium of some 250 or 300 insurance companies to insure the highest wind risk in the highest areas. It was the Florida Keys.

Ultimately, it was expanded to the Barrier Islands, but later on the industry wanted to basically take huge chunks of mainland and put all of the hurricane wind risk over into that pool instead of the companies themselves taking that risk, continuing that risk as they had borne for some period of time. When the Department of Insurance and legislature would not let that occur in the state of Florida, what we saw the course of time, with reinsurance reinvigorated because of active competition in the market forces, and given greater incentives to offset losses through the Florida hurricane catastrophic fund, we saw then the market for homeowners insurance come back to life.

What I want to make sure here is that there is not going to be any terrorism insurance come January 1, and that we are not suddenly dumping all of the terrorism risk away from the insurance industry, which clearly would be the nicest for the industry, but after all the insurance industry is in the business of insuring risk. So let us see if we can find this happy balance.

Now, I would like to have Mr. Keating from the National Taxpayers Union, how about you critiquing the Consumer Federation of America's plan, and critique the industry's plan.

Mr. KEATING. Well, I think the Consumer Federation of America plan is probably better than the plans advanced by the administration. Probably our key concern with the plan is that it would probably never disappear. There would not be more assumption of risk over time by the private sector. It is just kind of a loan program. It has its pluses, but we would like to see something with built-in incentives for the industry to monitor its risk, as Mr. Moss said. I would associate many of our beliefs and thoughts with what he said here at the hearing.

As far as the industry plan, I think they are mischaracterizing it to say that they were going to pay for federal reinsurance. At least the bill that I saw in its most recent draft, I think October 10, specifically excluded payment for federal reinsurance unless there were certain levels of capital. Maybe there is another bill that I have not seen since then, but that was the last one that I have seen, and I think that is a mischaracterization of the proposal to say it is always paid for, therefore, we could not support that approach.

Also, we could not support the idea that something would be chartered in a state, yet the federal government and the federal taxpayer is on the hook for the payments from the corporation. If there is going to be a federal backstop, or federal guarantee, we think there has to be federal oversight, instead of just state oversight.

Senator NELSON. So of the three plans, the administration plan, the Consumer Federation plan, and the industry's plan, you favor the Consumer Federation plan the best of the three?

Mr. KEATING. Of those three. Now, my written statement has another approach which we obviously would favor more than the others. That being said, I must say—and it sounds like Professor Moss has a plan, too, I would love to see.

Senator NELSON. I am getting to him.

Mr. KEATING. Perhaps he has come up with something better than what anyone else has proposed. I like his characterization of what we need to see, We need to see the right incentives to allow the private sector to come back in and manage these risks. They are going to do a better job than the federal government and the political system over time, and that is important not only for fiscal soundness, but for human life and property.

So these are all very important issues. I think our plan is probably superior to the others, but he may have one that is even better. We are open-minded about this.

Senator NELSON. Professor, share with us, and pull that mike over to you.

Mr. MOSS. I believe I know about all of the plans, I understand that reasonable people are trying to solve this problem, and I appreciate that very much. What I have tried to think about is the very simplest thing we could do, especially since time is of the essence, and it seemed to me that a very simple plan would be this: each insurer could be allowed to cede some level of terror risk, let us say, between 20 and 80 percent of its terror risk to the federal government; and whatever proportion of risk it chose to cede, it would be required to cede the same proportion of premium. That is the plan.

If you wanted to make it a little bit more complicated, if you wanted to inject a subsidy, you could reduce the amount of premium they cede by some percentage. But that is just a modest variation on the plan. It seems to me the advantage of this approach is that it would price the risk. You would allow the insurance industry to move these enormous risks and the enormous uncertainty off their books for the moment, but they would have to pay for it.

In fact, countries that have done this with natural disaster risk have seen that over time the industry decides—well, we start by wanting to cede all the risk it can, let us say 80 percent. But it does not take long for insurers to say, now, we would like to cede 70 percent, and over time 60, 50, and finally you get down to the bottom end. That is what we have seen in other countries that have done similar things.

So my sense is that this plan would—if not disappear altogether—it would recede over time on its own accord. Most importantly, I think it would essentially solve the problem at hand without distorting the market in some of the ways that the other plans might inadvertently do.

Senator NELSON. So your suggestion, you use the figures just as an example, 20/80, so you are talking about first dollar coverage?

Mr. MOSS. That is right.

Senator NELSON. So you are talking very close to the administration's plan?

Mr. MOSS. No, I do not think that is right. They charge a price of zero for government coverage. I think that is the critical mistake in the administration's plan. I think we should charge the full risk premium. The insurers can set whatever premium they want, but they have to cede a portion of that premium commensurate with the amount of risk they cede. If they cede 80 percent of the risk to the federal government, they should cede 80 percent of the premium. Therefore, they will have to charge a higher premium than if the government absorbed their risk for free.

Senator NELSON. And until we can determine what is an actuarially sound premium for that risk, what would, under your plan, determine that premium?

Mr. MOSS. My personal opinion is that the insurer is in the best position to set that premium, perhaps with some guidance from the state regulators. So I would let them set within some reasonable bounds any premium they would like to set, as long as they are willing to cede the portion of the premium that corresponds to the risk they are ceding to the federal government.

Now, I understand that may not be politically acceptable, and that there may need to be a deductible. If there is a deductible or retention of, say, $10 billion or $4 billion, or whatever the potential retention is, then the government would have to get in the business of setting the price and saying how much it is going to charge for the reinsurance.

I am a bit uncomfortable with that, which is why I would rather do this without a retention, without a deductible—essentially co-insurance. But I think if you did want a deductible or retention, we could try to work out the pricing. It would just be more complicated. My sense is we should just try to do the simplest possible thing, and that is what I have tried to propose.

Senator NELSON. Okay. Mr. Plunkett, would you critique that?

Mr. PLUNKETT. I think our assessment would be that his principles are correct, and very briefly I think we would say that we would like to see the details that he is looking at properly in terms of pricing and shifting risk as much as possible to an industry that is in fairly good financial shape.

Regarding first dollar coverage, if they do pay a premium, I think we would be less concerned. One of our guiding principles from the beginning has been actuarial soundness, and the basic tenet of actuarial soundness is that they pay something for the product that they are buying, and that the premium be equitably assessed. I think it has promise.

I think there are a number of proposals that—we are not wedded to our proposal as long as certain principles are met.

I would like to say, if I could, in response to the critique you heard of our plan, that it certainly does spread risk. For instance, above the retention that we propose in the 5 to 10 percent range based on the surplus of our company we are spreading the risk to the taxpayer, because they are loaning these companies money. Then above 10 percent you are spreading risk to all the ratepayers, because they will, through the surcharge on the state premium tax, pay whatever is loaned above 10 percent of losses back, and I might add that that in our opinion is a much fairer way in terms of apportioning risk to do it, because the folks who are paying the premiums, are obviously those who would assume the highest risk and are paying the highest premiums. Also, they will pay the most on the premium surcharge, and that is certainly a fairer way to do it, if you are requiring that loans be paid back, than to have it paid by taxpayers.

Senator NELSON. Professor, one thing that his plan does is that it, from the very first dollar in a very difficult determination of what should be the premium. Part of what Mr. Plunkett is saying is that in effect the consumer is not going to pay a premium unless there is a loss, and then that loss is passed on to the consumer, and the case was, he said, loans were made, and those loans were made or repaid over the course of 20 or 30 years, but those loans would not be made unless the terrorism loss occurred, which gives you a little more stability, because I think Mr. Nutter and Mr. Vagley have pointed out, how in the world do you determine what is an actuarially sound premium right now for the terrorism risk.

Mr. KEATING. May I comment on this plan briefly?

Senator NELSON. Yes, Mr. Keating.

Mr. KEATING. I like the plan very much as described here. I have to think about it some more and ask some of our advisors what they think about it, too. But my first impression is that one of the major strengths of this plan is that it keeps the incentives right, and that people who are pricing this product are going to have the most incentive to do as much research as possible to properly price this project to attempt, where possible, to avoid concentration of risk.

I mean, we are talking about covering a building that is a $4 billion building, no one should have a concentration of risk like that, and I would presume that you are going to see the risk chopped up into smaller pieces where people can digest them and price them, because across the country I do not think anyone is thinking our whole country is going to be destroyed by terrorist attack. We hope we do not see the kind of thing we saw in New York last month, but I think his proposal gets a lot of it right. I like it very much.

My only caution would be, if state regulators are somehow distorting the prices that might be charged, that could be a real problem in getting these prices set properly, so we would want to avoid the federal government—if the federal government is going to be taking a premium regulated by some State entity, that could pervert, I think, some of the very positive aspects of the proposal.

Mr. PLUNKETT. It absolutely is appropriate, and this is something we would want to look at carefully, and Professor Moss' proposal as well. If the government is picking up some portion of losses, it is absolutely appropriate to go through the states, because they regulate insurance, to look at affordability and accessibility. That is a key part of the concern for us, and it certainly would be appropriate in any of these proposals for the states to do that.

Now, we all understand it needs to be done quickly. We understand what the concern is with the policies expiring at the end of the year. I do not think anyone would suggest that lollygagging would be a good idea, but it certainly is absolutely appropriate.

Senator NELSON. And not to throw a monkey wrench into this thing, but we have not even discussed what are we going to do about business interruption insurance, so indeed, we have got to start working overtime to get this thing underway.

Well, I want to thank you for a most enlightening and most engaging panel to discuss a very difficult issue, and on behalf of our chairman and Ranking Member, Senator McCain, our Ranking Member, and Senator Hollings, our chairman, I want to thank you all very much for your participation.

The meeting is adjourned.

[Whereupon, at 5:10 p.m., the committee adjourned.]

APPENDIX

PREPARED STATEMENT ON BEHALF OF THE FOLLOWING ASSOCIATIONS AND THEIR MEMBERS:

AMERICAN COUNCIL FOR CAPITAL FORMATION
ASSOCIATED GENERAL CONTRACTORS OF AMERICA
AMERICAN RESORT DEVELOPMENT ASSOCIATION
BUILDING OWNERS AND MANAGERS ASSOCIATION INTERNATIONAL
INTERNATIONAL COUNCIL OF SHOPPING CENTERS
MORTGAGE BANKERS ASSOCIATION OF AMERICA
NATIONAL APARTMENT ASSOCIATION
NATIONAL ASSOCIATION OF INDUSTRIAL AND OFFICE PROPERTIES
NATIONAL ASSOCIATION OF REAL ESTATE INVESTMENT TRUSTS
NATIONAL ASSOCIATION OF REALTORS
NATIONAL MULTI HOUSING COUNCIL
PENSION REAL ESTATE ASSOCIATION
THE REAL ESTATE BOARD OF NEW YORK
THE REAL ESTATE ROUNDTABLE

Mr. Chairman, we commend you for the much-needed attention that you and the Committee are bringing to this important issue by holding a hearing today. It is clear that the Committee clearly recognizes the importance of this issue and its potential effect on the U.S. economy. We thank you for your leadership in addressing insurance-related problems as a result of the events of September 11, and we also appreciate the White House efforts to remedy a potential insurance coverage crisis. The real estate and construction industries, which account for over a quarter of the nation's gross domestic product, could face severe economic dislocation in the coming months if the federal government does not immediately address insurance-related issues tied to terrorism.

To continue to operate in the normal course of business, these industries need to continue to have insurance for risks that have traditionally been insurable, including damage associated with terrorism. The insurance industry recently testified before the full Committee that without Federal support, it will not be able to provide terrorism coverage in the future. Further, as the nation expands its mission against terrorism, the line between terrorism and war will likely become increasingly blurred from an insurance standpoint.

The Problem

On September 26, the CEOs of several major insurance companies testified before the House Financial Services Committee that the insurance industry expects to be able to pay claims associated with the September 11 terrorist attacks. However, they also said that insurers would not be able to provide terrorism coverage for future terrorist acts. The reason is that reinsurance for terrorist risks is generally unavailable in the current marketplace.

We take the insurance industry's warnings seriously and the Congress must as well. The lack of adequate reinsurance in the current market means that coverages our members need could very soon become unavailable to large segments of the U.S. economy. A significant percentage of owners of commercial properties open to the public, including shopping centers, offices, apartments and hotels, renew their insurance coverage on January 1 of each year. Many construction projects, including a number of new power plants, are slated to begin early and throughout next year. Many of the owners and developers already have been advised that their policies may not be renewed or that their new policies will exclude terror/war risks. Further, some owners have been advised that their current coverage may be terminated before their policies were set to expire, after the insurers provide the required advance notice (usually 90 days).

On October 15, a senior Bush Administration official said: "Without coverage against terrorist acts, banks will not lend to new construction; it will be difficult to sell major projects such as new pipelines, new power plants, skyscrapers. So we do think there is a problem that needs to be addressed." We could not agree more.

Mr. Chairman, the property owners among our members (including many pension funds that provide retirement security for their workers and families) cannot buy, sell, or finance the acquisition or construction of a commercial building unless it is covered by adequate insurance. Before September 11, adequate insurance was readily available. Neither property nor general liability policies in the U.S. excluded losses stemming from terrorist attacks. They excluded only acts of war. It now appears that terrorism coverage will not be available and that war risk coverage, which did not previously seem imperative, is now necessary to the extent any future attacks could be viewed as war-related.

The real estate and construction industries are leading pillars of the U.S. economy. Without adequate insurance, it will be difficult, if not impossible to operate or acquire properties, to construct new properties, to refinance loans, or sell commercial mortgage-backed securities (of which $350 billion is currently outstanding). Disappearance of coverage for terrorist acts could severely disrupt the U.S. economy.

The effects on our members of losing their insurance coverage are potentially severe. First, building owners and operators will be fully exposed to property damage losses from terrorist attacks and will be powerless to do anything about it. Worse, some state insurance regulators may not permit insurers to exclude terrorism coverage, raising the possibility that insurers will withdraw completely from such states and leave our members without any coverage at all.

Second, our members will also be exposed to third-party liability claims for terrorism and war risks. Without adequate insurance, they will be forced to choose between incurring these risks or closing their buildings to avoid them.

Third, virtually all of our members have clauses in their financing agreements requiring that minimum levels of insurance coverage on the property be in place. Without the required coverage, lenders would be free to foreclose because the loan would be in default without required insurance. Even more importantly, without adequate insurance coverage, lenders would not approve new loans to finance new construction or property sales, or refinance existing debt. This lack of liquidity could lead to the same severe problems the real estate and construction industries confronted after the savings and loans crisis when property values fell more than 30% largely because sources of capital dried up. Any similar liquidity crunch could have severe consequences on employment and state and local property and sales tax collections.

Further, portfolio lenders would be confronted with the possibility of limiting operations. The ability to finance commercial real estate transactions by institutional investors such as pension funds and life insurance companies would be at risk. These mortgage lenders have a fiduciary duty of prudence in investing money, and investing funds without adequate insurance would breach this duty. A lender refusing to make a loan without adequate insurance is not being arbitrary, it is acting in the best interest of the investor, whose money the lender is investing.

Fourth, the property owners among our members are likely to find that they cannot complete their construction projects, or begin new projects, until terrorism coverage can be restored. Lenders are unlikely to approve construction loans until our members can obtain builders risk insurance that is broad enough to cover acts of terrorism. This will affect not only our members, but also the U.S. economy as a whole. As you know, the construction industry is enormous and our economy was already struggling at the time of the terrorist attacks. The volume of construction that our members were putting into place had already begun to decline. Without government action to resolve this insurance problem, many construction workers are at risk of layoffs.

Fifth, apartment residents would see higher housing costs as real estate operating costs would increase significantly in the absence of continuing coverage of acts of terrorism. Even before September 11, multifamily owners and operators were facing year-over-year increases of 25–100% in their property and casualty insurance costs. Typically, these significant operating cost increases are reflected in higher market rents, especially in major urban markets with strong renter demand. In the absence of federal government involvement to provide for continuing coverage of terrorist acts, apartment renters, many of them low- and moderate-income families, will be forced to absorb a disproportionate share of heightened insurance costs and more-limited coverage. Federal government risk-sharing and the continued provision of coverage for acts of terrorism are needed to help moderate the impact on housing costs that renters will face as a result of the events of September 11.

Sixth, loss of coverage may lead to an increase in the cost of mortgage financing, especially in the commercial mortgage-backed securities (CMBS) market, as the result of an additional, difficult-to-quantify catastrophic risk to the real estate assets serving as security for the CMBS offerings. CMBS offerings are usually priced in the same manner as bonds and other fixed-income securities, heavily dependent on credit ratings issued by the major securities-ratings agencies. The rating agencies, and the fixed-income investment community in general, are very sensitive to any possible circumstances that could impair the cash flow available for payment of the securities in question. Of course, uninsured damage caused by terrorism could, as we have all seen, terminate, interrupt, or otherwise materially impair cash flow; that risk would loom particularly large to the extent that it is difficult to quantify.

An increase in the cost of mortgage financing could, in turn, cause otherwise viable projects not to be undertaken, and reduce income throughout the industry, leading to further lessening of demand and economic activity.

The war exclusions that have been included in our members' insurance policies for years mean that our members have always been exposed to losses resulting from acts of war. They cannot purchase war risk coverage separately in the market. This has not previously been a major concern because it was thought that the likelihood of losses related to acts of war on U.S. soil were quite remote. However, the events of September 11 and subsequent U.S. military activities in Afghanistan will cause the property owners among our members, and possibly their lenders, to reconsider whether it is acceptable to be exposed to such risks. The line between acts of war and acts of terrorism is in danger of blurring and our members cannot afford to be exposed to either risk. Henceforth, they must have adequate insurance protection for both risks. As of now they do not.

With many real estate businesses facing insurance policy cancellations and modifications on or before January 1, and both power plants and other construction projects ready to begin, the government must act now. Without government action, our industries will likely face the prospect of breaking promises to lenders, partners and others, of operating without necessary insurance coverage, and of watching the construction of new facilities slow down. Since operating a business without adequate insurance in many cases is not feasible, and is certainly unwise, real estate businesses will confront the possibility of ceasing or limiting operations until insurance once again becomes available. Without Federal action, the ability to finance, construct, buy or sell properties across the nation may be at risk.

Proposed Solution

We understand that the Committee will wish to ensure that the Federal government does not take action that will ultimately interfere with or displace the private insurance markets. We share that concern. However, it is not clear when, or if, the private insurance markets will be able to meet our members' needs for terrorist insurance coverage.

The Federal Government must play a role in ensuring that commercial property owners can continue to obtain coverage for damage for acts of terrorism. This is especially true in the near-term while we wait to see whether and how the private markets will adjust to the new post-September 11 realities and risks. Further, given the increasing possibility that a court could conclude that future damages caused by a terrorist actions is excludable as damages resulting from a state of war, the Government must also play a role, at least in a standby capacity, in ensuring the availability of coverage for damages arising from the actions undertaken by terrorists such as al Qaeda or their allies.

There is ample precedent for the Federal Government filling the insurance or reinsurance gap: (1) crime and riot insurance programs were created for urban business owners following the social unrest of the late 1960s and early 1970s; (2) flood and crop failures are insured under Federally sponsored programs; (3) standby war risk coverage already exists for certain aviation and maritime operations (including a post-September 11 expansion of the aviation war risk program); and (4) during World War II, the Government authorized a program, administered by private insurers, which insured property against "enemy attack."

The insurance industry has put forward a proposal to establish a special, state-chartered reinsurance company that would accept terrorist risks from companies wishing to cede risks to it. That company would then reinsure 95% of these terrorism risks to the federal government. That proposal builds upon a model in the United Kingdom where a special reinsurance pool for terrorist risks was created in the early 1990s in the wake of IRA bombings in the City of London. The U.K. Government provides a backstop to that pool, but has not been called upon to pay any losses to date.

The Bush Administration has outlined a proposal to deal with the current problem that would involve a three-year program under which the Federal Government and the insurance industry would share, in declining proportions each year, the risks of terrorist acts. While the details of this proposal must be made clear, including the scope of acts covered within the definition of terrorism, we believe it represents a positive step towards addressing this issue.

We commend both proposals to your careful consideration. In the end, however, we emphasize that the problem must be addressed in a satisfactory and timely manner. A critical criterion in measuring the effectiveness of any solution is whether the financial community will continue to provide capital necessary to buy, sell, construct or refinance properties. Since real estate is a long-lived asset, real estate financing tends to be long-term. Accordingly, the finite duration of federal involvement must not prevent lenders from making these long-term commitments. Further, the insurance industry's primary coverage should not be rendered immaterial by unrealistic retention amounts (*i.e.*, deductibles) imposed on insureds.

The Congress must not fail to act. The real estate and construction industries welcome the opportunity to work with the Administration and Congress to achieve a workable solution to this immediate problem this year. To discuss these issues in greater detail, please contact Tony Edwards at NAREIT at (202) 739–9400 or *tedwards@nareit.com* or Chip Rodgers at The Real Estate Roundtable at (202) 639–8400 or *crodgers@rer.org*.

○

APEX
TP
9780160735486
76901945-80